San Pablo Cave and El Cayo

on the

Usumacinta River, Chiapas, Mexico

PAPERS
of the
NEW WORLD ARCHAEOLOGICAL FOUNDATION

NUMBER FIFTY-THREE

San Pablo Cave and El Cayo
on the
Usumacinta River, Chiapas, Mexico

by
THOMAS A. LEE, JR.
and
BRIAN HAYDEN

with an appendix by
PHILLIP L. WALKER

NEW WORLD ARCHAEOLOGICAL FOUNDATION
BRIGHAM YOUNG UNIVERSITY
PROVO, UTAH
1988

Printed by
BRIGHAM YOUNG UNIVERSITY PRINT SERVICES
PROVO, UTAH

PREFACE

The data on which this report is based were collected by Lee during three rubber-raft trips down the Usumacinta River. The trips were planned and directed by Mr. Jack Curry of Western River Expeditions, Inc., Salt Lake City.

Archaeological expeditions into the upper Usumacinta River region, prior to the aviation era, followed an overland route from Tenosique, Tabasco, via Desempeño (near El Cayo, Chiapas) just above or at Porvenir, below the great ruins of Piedras Negras, Guatemala. This overland route was necessitated by the rapids, falls, and huge whirlpools characteristic of the stretch of river below Porvenir and above Tenosique, especially in the San José Canyon. The river there is too dangerous for native watercraft. The University of Pennsylvania Museum's project at Piedras Negras in 1931 and 1932 was forced to take the sixteen stelae removed from the site overland, by ox-drawn wagons on a road especially constructed for the move, to San José, where they used log rafts to float the stelae to Tenosique and Frontera. This was done to bypass the larger, more difficult rapids and sections of the San José Canyon and to run only the small, lowermost rapid (Mason 1934, 1935).

To our knowledge, until 1963 the Usumacinta had never been run completely from Tres Naciones, at the mouth of the Lacantun River, to Tenosique, Tabasco; it held little challenge, however, for the large rubber pontoon boats used on the Western River Expeditions trips.

The Lacandon Forest, through which the Usumacinta and its Mexican tributaries flow, scene of area-wide lumbering and chicle gathering from the middle of the last century up until the 1920s, was then much more accessible via overland trail than it has been since. The disappearance of these two intensive industries and the withdrawal of the thousands of men they employed left this area to the fate of the tropical forest which soon covered the trails, camp sites, and villages. The chicle industry used the rivers extensively for transportation along their navigable portions; only the lumber companies used the river throughout its entire length. Mahogany and cedar logs cut by the lumber companies were dragged to the riverbanks during the dry season, branded with the company's mark, and stacked to await the rains. When the water level rose with the advance of the rainy season, the logs were pushed into the river to float freely down the rapids of San José Canyon and to be collected and chained together in rafts below Boca del Cerro. These huge rafts were then towed to the coast, where the logs were loaded onto ocean-going freighters destined for international markets.

The middle Usumacinta River region, in terms of modern archaeological investigation and publication, is still little known due to its extreme difficulty of access. In 1963 any effort spent in archaeological reconnaissance combined with even limited testing was thought to be of considerable value in helping to unravel the cultural history of this important sector of the western Lowland Maya area.

As the NWAF was nearing completion of its Chiapa de Corzo and Izapa projects in 1963 and would soon be planning future research, I suggested to Mr. Curry that I would cooperate with his tours if the trips could be oriented towards archaeological reconnaissance. Such reconnaissance would supplement the few data collected by Gareth W. Lowe and Eduardo Martinez E. on an earlier and even briefer NWAF expedition into part of the same area in March, 1957 (Lowe 1959: 4–5).

The first two Western River Expeditions, Inc., trips originated at Tres Naciones at the mouth of the Lacantun River where all food, equipment, and personnel were flown in by B–18s and Cessna 180s from Tuxtla Gutiérrez. The first expedition spent ten days on the river (Nov. 12–22, 1964); the second was lengthened to twelve days (Nov. 29–Dec. 10, 1965). During the latter trip we were able to make small test excavations at San Pablo Cave, which had been discovered on the first trip. The destination of both expeditions and the take-out point was Tenosique, Tabasco.

A third river trip organized by Mr. Curry for December, 1969, to January, 1970, in which I also participated, started much farther upstream at San Quintin on the Jatate River and traversed the Colorado Canyon and the Lacantun River before cruising the upper and middle Usumacinta River sections traveled in the earlier two trips, and again ending at Tenosique. This trip was twenty-two days long, and, while one day was spent in the El Cayo region, no new archaeological excavations were undertaken. During this trip, however, general notes were made on the environment, flora, and fauna of the area immediately adjacent to El Cayo Island, and the San Pablo Cave and the El Cayo ceremonial center were again visited. A general archaeological reconnaissance was carried out during the entire trip, although no ceramics or other cultural materials were collected.

ACKNOWLEDGMENTS

It is obvious from the above how much we owe to Jack L. Curry and his Western River Expeditions, Inc. for facilitating the archaeological work carried out in the El Cayo area. It is a pleasure to thank him here for his friendship and his financial support of this research. It can truly be said that without his equipment and organizational ability this research would never have been initiated or carried out. Gareth W. Lowe, director of the NWAF, encouraged my participation.

Mexican government permits for reconnaissance and limited test excavations were provided first by the late archaeologist Jorge R. Acosta and later by archaeologist José Luis Lorenzo, of the Dirección de Monumentos Prehispánicos of the Instituto Nacional de Antropología e Historia, for the years in which the first two trips were made. Without the cooperation of these individuals this research would not have been possible.

The lithic analysis is the work of Brian Hayden of Simon Fraser University, who willingly crowded it into his already overloaded schedule during an analysis of the colonial lithics of Coneta, Chiapas. His good will and cheerful attitude are greatly appreciated.

We especially wish to thank Joseph W. Ball for his interest in the ceramics from San Pablo Cave and for his type-variety identifications of all ceramics that are formally named in this report. Lawrence Feldman identified the freshwater and land snail shells.

The finished maps, plans, and sections are the work of José Nuñez based on my pencil drawings. The artifact drawings are by Ramiro Jimenez Pozo and Jennifer Taschek Ball. Photographs in the studio and darkroom are the work of Mario Vega Roman and Douglas Donne Bryant. Each of these individuals, especially Taschek Ball, has contributed significantly to the visual aspect of this report.

We are very appreciative of the collaboration of Phillip L. Walker who also on short notice took on the study of both the human and animal skeletal remains from the El Cayo zone. His careful analysis of this material is presented in Appendix A.

More than thirty *compañeros* on the first two trips sweated uncomplainingly in the toil of opening trails through almost impenetrable river-edge jungle, wilted in the heat and humidity, shivered in the cold of a sudden tropical night rain squall, and shared the few archaeological joys of the trips. The experience of suddenly recognizing, in a sea of green vegetation, the long lost community of some ancient Maya group, was one highly appreciated by all. We thank each of these associates for his or her aid in the daily tasks of an archaeological reconnaissance made under difficult conditions and for long hours spent bent over, trowelling on the screens at the San Pablo Cave test excavations.

T. A. Lee, Jr.
San Cristóbal de Las Casas, Chiapas

CONTENTS

FIGURES

TABLES

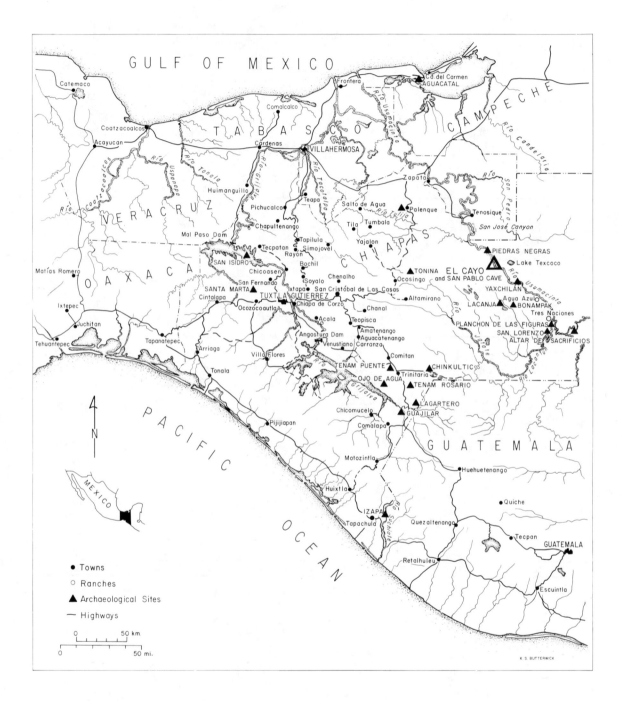

Figure 1.   MAP OF CHIAPAS AND ADJACENT AREAS SHOWING THE LOCATION OF EL CAYO RUINS,
SAN PABLO CAVE, AND RELATED SITES.

THE EL CAYO ARCHAEOLOGICAL ZONE AND INVESTIGATIONS

ENVIRONMENT

Physiography

Approximately 37 km downstream from the large Classic Maya site of Yaxchilan the Usumacinta River divides into two branches during high water around the small island of El Cayo (Fig. 1). The upstream end of this island has been built up with tons of pebbles of many colors; it marks the exit of the Usumacinta River from the hilly country through which it has flowed for about 80 km. About 1 km below the island the river again enters high hills through which it flows for the next 70 km to Boca del Cerro in Tabasco. During low water a broad peninsula connects El Cayo Island to the right, or Guatemalan, bank of the river. A small stream which drains the large Lacandon Lake enters the Usumacinta just above the island on the same side of the river.

According to Maler (1903: 83, *footnote*) El Cayo means "the place where the banks are strewn with stones. Cayo is one of the words brought by the Spanish from Hayti and Cuba." His description upon arriving is of considerable interest:

We reached El Cayo on May 20th. Here, too, the view afforded a magnificent panorama. Emerging from the wild, cleft mountain, the river flows around an island covered with trees and forms an extensive beach, gleaming white in the sun, composed of sand and of broken stones ground smooth. Here the mineralogist can gather an interesting collection containing specimens of all that is buried in the heart of the most distant mountains of Chiapas and Guatemala. Many of these stones are so beautiful that even the natives never fail to take specimens, which they use as paperweights. Many species of stones are found here. I thought I recognized carnelian, syenite, jadeite, ofite,

hematite, pure white marble of the finest grain, very pretty pieces of petrified wood, etc. These stones, the most of which are extremely hard, are of all colors, white, ash gray, black, brown, ochre yellow, green, blood red, and pink. Many are striped with several colors . . . (Maler 1903: 84).

On the right bank the relatively flat terrain stretches northward into the Peten forest of Guatemala. On the left bank a small flat embayment in the mountains is interrupted by a high hill in its center near the margin of the river (Fig. 2). San Pablo Cave is located on the south side of this hill.

El Cayo lies in what Müllerried (1957, Map 4) has named the eastern mountain region of Chiapas, more commonly known as the Lacandon Forest. These mountains, varying in height from 90 m above sea level on the middle Usumacinta River to 1,200 m southeast of the Jatate River, run roughly northwest to southeast. The mountainous region varies from 70 to 100 km in width and is 150 km long (Müllerried 1957: 20–21). The general altitude of the hills parallel to the course of the Usumacinta River near El Cayo is 500 m above sea level, and the hilly zone is 10 to 15 km wide. This low range of hills separates the parallel valleys of the Usumacinta and Lacanja. The famous Classic Maya sites of Yaxchilan and Bonampak are found in the Usumacinta and Lacanja Valleys, respectively.

The eastern mountains consist of marine limestone strata in parallel fault blocks of Upper Mesozoic and Lower and Middle Tertiary age (Müllerried 1957: 116, 118). The most common strata on the surface throughout the region are of Paleocene, Eocene, Oligocene, and Lower and Middle Miocene age. Superficial deposits of Pliocene(?) and Quarternary times are widespread. Lateritic soils are the most common throughout the region due to the prevailing high rainfall and temperature.

a

b

Figure 2.   AERIAL VIEWS OF EL CAYO
Seen at low water; during high water El Cayo island is isolated from the Guatemalan shore, seen here at the upper right.
In these views the island is a clump of high vegetation surrounded by a sand and pebble beach. The river flows toward the
upper left. *a*. Wide view of the El Cayo vicinity. *b*. Close-up view of the El Cayo island and immediate environs;
San Pablo Cave is in the hillside facing the viewer in the left foreground.

Hydrology

The Usumacinta River system is so well known that it needs little introduction (Fig. 3). It is the largest river system in Mexico, with a drainage basin of 48,043 km² above Boca del Cerro, near Tenosique, Tabasco (Echeagaray Bablot 1957: 79; Compañ Pulido 1956). The waters rise in the Chiapas Highlands and the highland ranges of Guatemala and they empty into the Gulf of Mexico. Many maps and locally obtained data on the Usumacinta have been published by Compañ Pulido (1956).

The section of the river in which El Cayo lies (called by Maler the Central Usumacinta between the rapids of Anaite and Boca del Cerro) is deep and narrowly contained by steep hillsides. Near the lower reaches it forces its way between sheer limestone canyon walls (Fig. 4). The Central Usumacinta is not considered to be normally navigable in dugout canoes. The rapids of Anaite at the head and the San José rapids at the foot of this section of the river effectively close it to

practical navigation. There are significant sections between these two rapids, however, which are navigable, from above El Cayo to well below the ruins of Piedras Negras (Fig. 5).

Climate

The El Cayo area is well within the borders of the humid tropical climate, receiving an annual rainfall of 1,500–2,000 mm. The temperature minimum ranges between 8° and 10° C with a maximum variation from 40° to 42° C. The annual median temperature varies between 24° and 25° C, but there are as many as eight months of the year (Mar.–Sept.) which exceed the 25° C figure (Echeagaray Bablot et al. 1957: 1, Figs. 7, 8; Echeagaray Bablot 1957, Fig. 40, *below*).

An important factor in the local environment of any area is the evaporation rate. Since it expresses the interdependent relationship of rainfall, temperature, and wind, the rate of evaporation is also a good index of expectable vegetation, reflecting the relative humidity in the area. El

Figure 3.   THE ANAITE RAPIDS BELOW AGUA AZUL

Figure 4.   AERIAL VIEW OF THE SAN JOSÉ CANYON

Figure 5.   TYPICAL DUGOUT CANOE ON THE USUMACINTA RIVER

Cayo is in an area which has an annual average evaporation of 1,300 to 1,500 mm (Echeagaray Bablot et al. 1957: 1, Fig. 9). The figure of 1,300 mm is the lowest known evaporation rate in southeastern Mexico and is indicative of the high, always green tropical forest vegetation which is found there.

In the Köeppen climatic classification, the region is labeled Afwg and is characterized by a humid, tropical type of forest vegetation with maximum rains in the fall and the annual temperature maximum occurring before the summer solstice.

Although the evaporation rate suggests that the local winds are minimal, El Cayo is in the area affected in the summer and early fall by cyclones that originate in the Caribbean Sea and come sweeping in, generally over Belize and across the Peten, into and across the Lacandon Forest, and out across Tabasco to the Gulf of Mexico. While these often reach a destructive magnitude, they carry along super-charged humid conditions which greatly augment the long-range pattern of rainfall. El Cayo does not normally suffer because of this extra rainfall, as the local topography drains well. The same cannot be said for the nearby, flat, low-lying Tabascan Lower Usumacinta Basin, however, where even the normal year's runoff causes destructive flooding. Years with cyclonic storms always result there in high property damage and loss of livestock and even human lives.

The commonly conceived ideas about "jungles" or tropical forests being hot, humid, and literally steaming during the day and bitter cold in the early morning hours just before and after daybreak, holds true for the Upper Usumacinta Region. During the summer, fall, and winter a few days may be unbearably hot and humid, but they are often followed by a *norte* of low cloud cover and cold dripping rain of several days' duration. The drastically changeable climate of the Lacandon Forest is one of the principal reasons that it has historically been considered an unhealthy place. Although the Classic Maya seem to have found it a suitable habitat, they nevertheless had to overcome an environment which to our point of view is anything but hospitable.

Flora

The area around Group A, south of San Pablo Cave, is the most dense, second-growth cane I have ever tried to penetrate! Reconnaissance on foot there was begun with *machetes* by cutting, from the front of the rubber rafts, first a landing place on the steep left river margin and then tunnels inland in order to reconnoiter the area. The cane, so interwoven and matted that it refused to fall when cut off at the bottom and along both sides, had to be cut off above also. Only after carefully cutting the central, free-standing mass again and again could one finally begin to mash it down onto the tunnel floor, only to begin the whole process again, and, thus, slowly, meter by meter, cut one's way inland. This particular section of the El Cayo zone seems to be secondary growth, although there is no evidence of an earlier high forest. The presence of permanent pre-Hispanic habitation eliminates the possibility that the entire area is a flood plain which would explain the absence of a high forest over part of it. A high forest would have limited the cane growth to only the very edge of the river. This brings us to another independent factor affecting vegetation growth, that is, sunlight.

Contrary to popular belief, a high tropical forest is not thick or dense on the ground, but open, with just a few tree trunks and leafless vines to hinder progress along the forest floor. The lack of sunlight below the upper canopy of a high forest seriously restricts the lower vegetation growth. Only where the sunlight is strong and constant, along river and stream banks, in clearings in the forest where large old trees have fallen leaving an open hole in the canopy, and in abandoned cornfields, does the vegetation grow thick and almost impenetrable. Once past the dense perimeters of a high forest, one can move quite freely, only cutting here and there at an occasional vine which impedes one's progress.

No attempt will be made here to describe in detail the flora of the El Cayo zone. For those who wish to pursue this aspect further I recommend Wagner (1964: 224-228) for a general description of the Chiapas rain forest, and Miranda (1952, 1953) and Echeagaray Bablot et al. (1957: 1, 77, 85–88) for more specialized treatments.

Many tropical species of orchids are discussed by Hartman (1971). A bleak picture of the current destruction of the Lacandon Forest, which is proceeding at an alarming rate, with an impassioned plea from a concerned conservationist is to be found in Duby (1974).

The always-green high forest, the vegetation zone in which El Cayo falls, ranges from 30 to 70 m in height (Figs. 6 and 7). This zone is characterized by tree species which occur in great abundance. Some of the better known are mahogany (*Swietenia macrophylla* King), cedar (*Cedrela mexicana* Roem), *mulato* (*Vatairea lundellii*), *canxan* (*Terminalia abovaton* Stand), *chicozapote* or *chicle* (*Achras zapote* L.), and *ceiba* (*Ceiba pentandra* Gaertn). Many smaller arboral species as vines, parasites, aerophites, ferns, and others are found in their particular ecological niches among the larger trees. A good discussion of forest resources in the Lacandon Forest may be found in Martinez Vasquez (1974).

Fauna

The term "jungle" or tropical forest, for most people calls to mind the fauna characteristic of it.

The jaguar (*Felis onca*), the crocodile (*Crocodilus americanus*), the tapir (*Tapirella bairdii*), the *tepescuintle* or *agouti* (*Agouti paca uisgata*), the *javelina* (*Tayassu angulatus*), and the boa (*Constrictor constrictor*), as well as other more exotic mammal and reptile species. Among the most typical birds of the area are the red macaw (*Ara macao*), the blue-headed parrot (*Autumnalis faironsa*), the *chachalaca* (*Ortalis vetula*), the *faisan real* (*Crax rubra rubra*), and the *cojolite* (*Penelope purpuraseens*).

For more information on the reptiles of this area the reader is referred to Alvarez del Toro (1960). Another good general book by the same author covers the most characteristic wild animals of Chiapas (Alvarez del Toro 1952). Regarding avifauna, much detailed information is found in Alvarez del Toro (1963, 1964, 1971). Velasco Colin (1976) describes the freshwater fishes of Chiapas.

PRESENT-DAY HUMAN HABITATION ALONG THE RIVER

In 1963, on my first trip down the Usumacinta River, the human population was located at

Figure 6.   VEGETATION ALONG THE BANKS OF THE USUMACINTA RIVER

three places on the Mexican side and only two on the Guatemalan side (Fig. 8):

It was impossible to visit more sites because of the lack of time and guides who knew the area intimately. The area is replete with wild animals, but from Tres Naciones to Boca del Cerro there are only an estimated 80 people living along the river. The reason for the lack of trails and other lines of communication becomes more apparent when it is realized that all these people live in three widely separated spots in the Upper Usumacinta Valley. In the lower half of the valley there simply are no inhabitants (Lee 1963).

The three settlements were Tres Naciones at the mouth of the Lacantun River, Agua Azul some 23 km more or less downriver on the Usumacinta River, and the four de la Cruz families at Yaxchilan farther downstream (Fig. 9).

During the second trip we found a new water-measuring station with two families just below Tres Naciones on the Mexican side, a few widely scattered houses on the Guatemalan side,

five Lacandon women living alone just above El Cayo Island, and a few new houses on the Mexican side just above Boca del Cerro (Lee 1969). The Lacandon women (grandmother, mother, and daughter with her two small daughters) had moved there within the year from Lake Texcoco, about two miles to the east in Guatemala, after the two male members of the family (husbands of the mother and the daughter) had died of unknown diseases. Only the daughter was communicative, saying that the others only spoke *Caribe*. They had made a *milpa* which had produced well, she said, and their patio was full of chickens, turkeys, and pigs. All in all they seemed to be doing well. Below El Cayo in 1965 there were a few more houses, but only near Boca del Cerro on the Mexican side of the river.

Our experience through the same Usumacinta River section during the third trip (Dec. 1969–Jan. 1970) was very different. On the Guatemalan side, after leaving Tres Naciones, we were rarely out of sight of houses. Small settlements had formed on the right bank opposite Agua Azul and especially in front of Yaxchilan. Below the rapids of Anaite, however, there were no new houses.

Figure 7.   TALL RAIN FOREST IN THE EL CAYO REGION

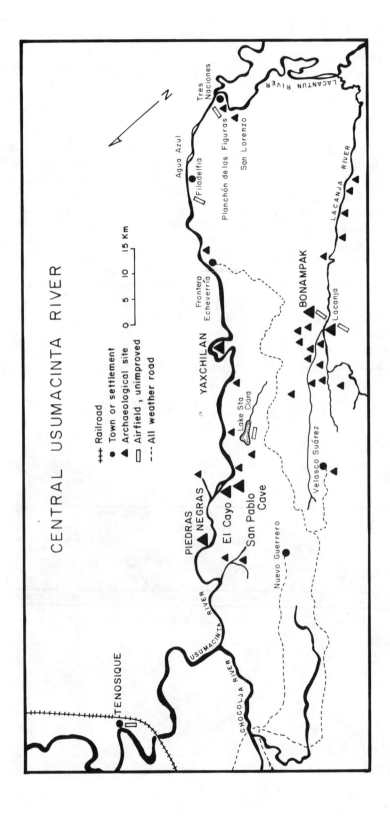

Figure 8.   MAP OF THE CENTRAL USUMACINTA RIVER
(from Blom 1953 and S. P. P. n.d.)

Figure 9. PATIO AND TYPICAL HOUSES AT AGUA AZUL, CENTRAL USUMACINTA REGION

On the Mexican or left bank new ranches had been started between Tres Naciones and Agua Azul, between Agua Azul and Yaxchilan, and even at El Cayo itself. We found the ceremonial center partially cleared and the area north of it to a small arroyo which drains the embayment, about 500 m away, had been planted with grass for cattle. A rude tin-roofed house had been built and a small airstrip developed. A couple of cowboys lived there and were supplied by air from Tenosique by the ranch owner.

Although we did not visit the Lacandon family across the river from El Cayo, smoke rising through a thatch roof there signaled their continued presence.

On the Mexican side there were no speakers of indigenous languages at any of the ranches or settlements in 1970. On the Guatemalan side I can only point to the Lacandon family at El Cayo as indigenous. There may well have been Maya people other than Lacandons in the ranches and settlements on the Guatemalan side, but we purposefully refrained from entering the country.

Only near Boca del Cerro, below El Cayo, could one see the rapid process of deforestation that accompanies any new settlement. This is a process, which, within a few years, will leave no part of the Usumacinta River Basin forest untouched by the hand and axe of modern man.

PRESENT-DAY SETTLEMENT AND LAND USE

The decade of the 1970s brought many changes to the Lacandon Forest in general, particularly along those portions of the Usumacinta River where the terrain is flatter. The few Lacandon Indians of the 1960s have multiplied to more than 400. Their land rights, threatened by invading Indian and *mestizo* farmers, were secured by presidential decree in 1981 which set aside 614,321 ha for the sole use of sixty-six families in Naja, Metzaboc, Zapote Caribal, and Lacanja Chansayoba (Robles 1982: 206). This has resulted in a situation which will be explosive in the future since now 0.6 percent of the population has legal title to 40 percent of the land (ibid).

An all-weather inland lumber road reaching deep into the area starts at Penjamo, Tabasco, near Boca del Cerro, and parallels the middle section of the Usumacinta well away from the river. During the dry season, one can now (1981) drive into Bonampak with good luck. The road extends more than 35 km beyond by a different fork to Colonia Frontera Echeverria up river from Yaxchilan at the old *montera* of Filadelfia. And so it will continue as long as the populations of the Chiapas Highlands continue to expand in an almost explosive rate and there continues to exist uncut forest with even marginal soils beneath it to plant on.

Lumber contracts for mahogany and cedar have been signed by the Lacandons, the proceeds of which have allowed them to buy trucks and buses which carry them daily to outside markets to sell their arts and crafts, particularly sets of bows and arrows. Recent *ladino* immigrations into the area have been forcefully congregated into two large communities: Frontera Echeverria (Corozal) and Dr. Manuel Velasco Suarez (Palestina). The former, a few kilometers downstream from Filadelfia, has a Tzeltal and Tzotzil population of about 7,000 divided into thirteen *barrios*. The latter community is located a little over 10 km east of the Ocotal lakes and consists of about 3,000 Chols in eight barrios (Pablo Ramirez Suarez, personal communication, 1985). The all-weather gravel road mentioned above connects these towns and intervening areas with Palenque, Chiapas, and Penjamo, Tabasco.

The wide band of hills parallel to the left bank of the Usumacinta River below Yaxchilan has been little affected by the "progress" seen in the interior valleys. No roads penetrate this area yet, nor were new signs of habitation along the river seen above the Budsilja River on a recent (Feb. 1982) flight over the area.

ARCHAEOLOGICAL RESEARCH IN THE EL CAYO REGION

EARLY EXPLORATIONS

The El Cayo ruins were first reported by Teobert Maler (1903: 83–89), who visited them in the spring of 1897, naming the ruins the Temple of the Five Temples (Fig. 10). Maler had spent one night in the montera, or forest camp, of El Cayo earlier in 1895. While there, he asked for and received information about ruined "cities;" Piedras Negras, however, was the only one which he names specifically (Maler 1901: 40). The El Cayo site was not discovered until later due to the thick vegetation, though it was not over 200 m away from the El Cayo montera (Maler 1903: 84).

During the week that Maler was at El Cayo (Group C) in 1897 he discovered three carved stelae (two with glyphs), a round altar, and a beautifully carved lintel with over one hundred well-preserved glyphs (Maler 1903: 84–89). He photographed Stelae 1 and 2 and Lintel 1, and drew Stela 3. He also made a plan, section, and reconstruction drawing of the facade of the Temple of the Five Temples. A graffito on another lintel was recorded also; Maler (1903, Fig. 27) called it a large St. Andrew's Cross, and he found others at Piedras Negras, La Mar, and San Lorenzo. The best three of the carved glyphic monuments of El Cayo were subsequently stolen, as detailed below. Maler's photographs were excellent and they are the only evidence we have of these beautiful monuments until they surface somewhere as part of a museum or private collection.

Dr. M. Wells Jakeman, then chairman of the Department of Archaeology, Brigham Young University, tried to reach El Cayo in 1954 but was unsuccessful because of a lack of time and money. Jakeman's report to the Instituto Nacional de Antropología e Historia, dated June 7, 1954, states:

> . . . however, on the return flight from Agua Azul, our pilot had obliged us by circling low over the El Chile-El Cayo area, providing us with a close-up study of that region which I hoped might result in the location of other sites. This air reconnaissance was successful. At one point near the river, we observed a large group of small hills which on further study proved to be arranged in an artificial manner, and in some cases seemed to be stepped . . . .

Later, in 1956, Jakeman reached El Cayo and he dug some test trenches. It has been reported that this expedition into the Central Usumacinta region

> . . . was a further, on-the-ground exploration of the site located in the aerial reconnaissance of 1954. Some of the ruined buildings were examined and test-trenching was carried out to determine the age of this ancient city. A sketch map of the ruins, field notes, photographs, and sherd material were brought back for further study, and for the planning of future large-scale excavations at the site . . . (Christensen 1956: 34.01).

The results of this second expedition have not been published, nor does there appear to have been a report made to the Instituto Nacional de Antropología e Historia.

In 1957, Gareth W. Lowe and Eduardo Martinez E. briefly visited the El Cayo zone.

> . . . later in the month of March, I was accompanied by Martinez on a flight to Agua Azul, on the Usumacinta River . . . From here a quick boat trip . . . took us downstream to the huge Maya site of Yaxchilan. . . . Leaving Yaxchilan, the boatmen were kind enough to take us downstream by dugout canoe as far as El Desempeño. A portage at the rapids of El Chile and El Anaite . . . had to be made, but otherwise, the trip down this storied river was rapid and full of interest. A brief inspection of El Cayo confirmed the fact of the Preclassic occupation of this other-

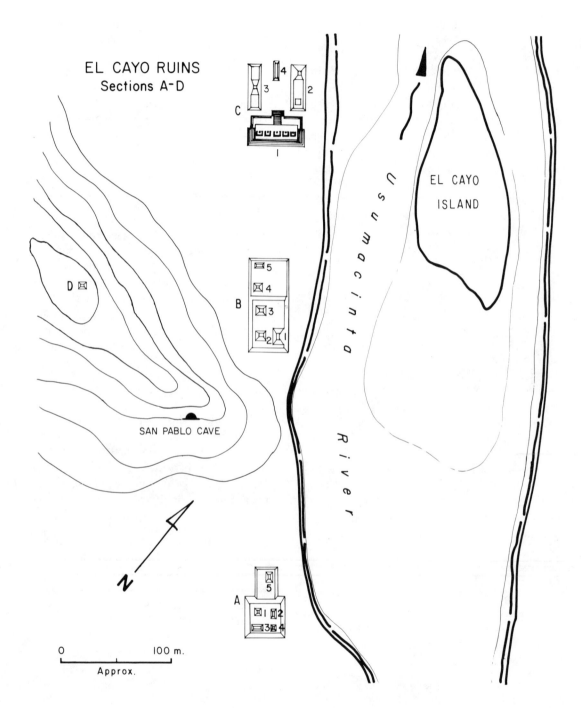

Figure 10.   MAP OF THE EL CAYO AREA AND IMMEDIATE ENVIRONS OF SAN PABLO CAVE

wise Classic Maya site. Landing on the Guatemalan side of the river, we then followed a newly-bulldozed timber trail to the airfield and lumber camp at Lake Texcoco. From this point, a two-day hike through the forest brought us back to our point of departure at Tenosique . . . (Lowe 1959: 4–5).

An attempt was made in the spring of 1962 by Bruce W. Warren, the late Maximo Prado (both then of the NWAF staff), and Ross T. Christensen (Department of Archaeology, BYU) to reach El Cayo overland from the colony of Santo Domingo, 18 km to the west of the Usumacinta River. This attempt was ill-fated from the beginning because no trails existed. After several days of cutting a new trail through dense forest the effort was abandoned when the time allowed ran out.

THE 1963 AND 1965 EXPLORATIONS

On the 1963 Western River Expeditions, Inc., river trip we spent two days pleasantly camped on the island of El Cayo while we reconnoitered the zone (Fig. 11).

The El Cayo archaeological site is located on the Mexican side of the river, due southeast of Lake Texcoco, Guatemala. The name of the site applies only to the most northern group of mounds (Maler's Temple of the Five Temples) and their associated plazas (Fig. 10, Group C). There is a general embayment in the mountains flanking the left bank in which several groups or clusters of mounds may be distinguished through the very thick but low secondary vegetation; I was not able to reach all the mounds in the short time available. I describe in detail in the architectural section only those areas which I personally visited.

During the 1963 trip, two days were spent reconnoitering the left, or Mexican, side of the river. The first morning one of the three survey parties located the cave, which we named San Pablo, on the south slope of the high hill next to the river in the center of the embayment (Fig. 12). That afternoon a surface collection (E-4) was made and most of the next day was spent excavat-

Figure 11.   PART OF THE 1963 CAMP ON EL CAYO ISLAND

Figure 12.   MEMBERS OF THE 1965 EXPEDITION IN THE ENTRANCE OF SAN PABLO CAVE

ing a 2m by 2m test pit (Excavation Unit A) at the north end of the cave near the west wall. No natural stratigraphy was noted, but sherds and lithic artifacts were very plentiful.

In 1964, Richard MacNeish, while visiting the NWAF's field laboratory in Tuxtla Gutierrez, Chiapas, reviewed the material from the 1963 test pit with me. He considered the material to be important, saying that "... some of the chipped stone types have not been made since 5,000 B.C. ... ," thus indicating that the cave apparently had a preceramic occupation. Since there were then no known artifacts for the Lowland Maya of so early a date, he urged that further excavations be made at San Pablo Cave if at all possible (Lee 1969: 1).

As mentioned above, the El Cayo region was inaccessible except by river from Tres Naciones or Agua Azul, a long and difficult journey. There had been no opportunity to re-enter this area

until I was again contacted by Jack Curry early in 1965 to see if I would be interested in accompanying him on another trip down the Usumacinta River. He added that I could plan to spend five to seven days in any area I chose along the river. I immediately thought of San Pablo Cave and MacNeish's recommendations. The Mexican Federal Electrical Comission was at that time drilling test holes downstream in the Boca del Cerro area near Tenosique in their search for a new hydroelectric dam site which, if built, might flood the El Cayo region and San Pablo Cave.

During the 1965 trip we dug and screened Sections I and II of Excavation Unit B. The sections were excavated in 20 cm levels and screened through 5 mm mesh. Three human burials and one "tomb" were found in these sections of the excavation. A description of both the 1963 and 1965 excavations in San Pablo Cave is given below.

SURFACE SURVEY OF THE EL CAYO REGION

Group A

This small but high square platform supports Structures 1–4; a lower platform appended to its north side supports the low Structure 5 (Fig. 10). All the superstructures have collapsed into large piles of rock. Structure 1 is 2 m high; Structure 3 is 3 m high. The height of the basal platform is about 4 m, while the platform appended to the north side is only half as high. Total height is about 7 m at the top of the southeasternmost structure. No stucco fragments were found. Sherds were not visible on the surface due to the heavy cane growth which covered this part of the site.

Group B

This group is situated almost opposite the island of El Cayo, just north of the point of the large hill that is so prominent in the El Cayo embayment. The group consists of a large basal platform bearing Structures 1–3 and a basal platform projecting northward with Structures 4 and 5 in ruins. The maximum height of this unit is not over 3 m. Only four surface sherds were collected on the northwest side of the basal platform mid-way between Superstructures 2 and 3 (Group B, Sample ECR-1; Table 1). A second surface sample of three sherds came from the northwest side of Superstructure 4 (Group B, Sample ECR-2; Table 1).

Group C

The northernmost part of the El Cayo ceremonial center and the most elaborate of the zone, this group consists of four principal structures and is the part that Maler (1903) originally reported.

Structure 1

Five north-facing temples on the summit of a single, large, high pyramidal platform constitute Maler's Temple of the Five Temples. This structure now has a total height of about 12.5 m. The platform has appended to its north side a basal platform surmounted by a secondary platform and a central stairway creating a "stage" on the front of the platform of the Five Temples.

Along the front of the platform of the Five Temples and on the top of the appended platform or stage is a series of at least four corbel-vaulted chambers, all of which by now have been badly damaged by pothunters.

The temple walls on top of the pyramid are about 1 m thick and are of coarse limestone block veneer with rubble and mortar fill. The walls of the central Temple 3 are still standing to a height of 2 m (Fig. 13). A very weathered carved stone portraying a complete human figure in profile (Maler's Stela 3) is still in the central temple. The stone (1.45 m long, 58 cm wide, and 20 cm thick) probably is a lintel. A sample of stucco relief decoration (Group C) was collected from among the fallen wall and roof comb debris within Temple 3 (Fig. 32). A sherd sample from a pothunter's hole within Temple 3 was also collected (Group C, Sample ECR-6; Table 1). For a more detailed description of this five-temple structure, see Maler (1903: 84–89).

One sample of shell, animal bone, and ceramics (Group C, Sample ECR-3; Table 1) was collected from the looters' backdirt inside and just outside of the corbel-vaulted room nearest the river (Temple 5). A second sample (Group C, Sample ECR-7; Table 1) of human and animal bone and ceramics was taken from the same backdirt but much lower down, at the level of the plaza. Another large pothunter's hole had been made about mid-way up the central stairway above the tier of vaulted rooms.

Structure 2

On the east or river side of the plaza north of Structure 1 (Structures 1 and 2 are separated by only a short distance), Structure 2 is a long, rectangular, low basal platform about 40 m long, 15 m wide, and 3 m high. On top of the platform is a small 5 m high secondary pyramid at the north end and a low rectangular structure at the south end. A few sherds were collected from the surface of Structure 2 (ECR-5; Table 1).

Structure 3

Across the plaza, 20 m away and parallel to Structure 2, this is another long platform also

Figure 13.   TEMPLE 3, STRUCTURE 1, EL CAYO

about 40 m long and 4 m high with a small 8 m high pyramid in the middle (ECR-4; Table 1).

Structure 4

Between Structures 2 and 3 at the north end of the plaza and parallel to them is a 20 m long, low and narrow primary platform which partially encloses the north end of the plaza. This plat-form, only about 1 m high and 5 m wide, has no visible superstructures. The lack of fallen rubble also suggests that if there had been a superstruc-ture on the platform, it was of a perishable na-ture.

About 200 m to the southwest, at the foot of the El Cayo hill, is a 3 m high platform that is 20 m wide and 50 m long.

Carved Monuments

Only two stone monuments remain of the five seen by Maler (1903: 85–89) in 1879. The two best stelae and the beautiful lintel were stolen some years ago (in about 1961) according to INAH guards at Yaxchilan. Those stones are Maler's Stelae 1 and 2 and Lintel 1 (Maler 1903, Pls. 34, 35). Only the plain round altar in the plaza in front of the main structure and the badly weathered lintel in the central temple on top (Maler's 1903, Fig. 31 Stela 3) remain of the monuments that he photographed. For a correlation of carved monument names, numbers, and dates as used by Maler (1903), Greene, Rands, and Graham (1972), Proskouriakoff (1950), and others, see Table 12.

Group D

This group consists of a single, small, square primary platform on top of the large central hill southwest of Group C. Of poorly preserved stone masonry, it is roughly 10 m² and about 2 m high.

San Pablo Cave

The cave was found by Paul Thevanin, boatman on the 1963 Usumacinta trip. On the morning of November 18th, I had divided our party into three groups, each one to reconnoiter a different sector of the large hill on the left bank of the Usumacinta River. The first group was to go around the south side of the hill, the second over the top, and the third around the north side. The first group, led by Mr. Thevanin, located the cave, which later was named San Pablo; the second group located Group D on top of the hill, and I in the third group located Groups B and C. A small surface sample (San Pablo Sample SPC-F, 1963; Table 1) of ceramics and chipped stone was collected from the cave floor.

In the afternoon, I returned to the cave to evaluate the deposit reported in the morning. A second, somewhat larger, surface collection was made at that time (San Pablo Sample SPC-4; Table 1). I decided that the prospects were good since the surface was dry and littered with worked stone, bone, and broken pottery. The "feel" from thumping suggested that there was a

meter or more of depth and that a test pit would be of some value. The next day, a 2 m by 2 m pit was dug near some large pieces of bedrock showing through the deposit at the rear of the cave and to the left of the center as one faces the cave (Fig. 14). Four 20 cm levels were excavated to bedrock. Further discriptions of this pit (Excavation Unit A) and its contents are presented below.

EXCAVATIONS IN SAN PABLO CAVE

Description of the Cave

San Pablo Cave is situated not more than 70 m from the left bank of the Usumacinta River, about 30 m up a steep talus slope at the front of a highly-weathered limestone cliff with a southern exposure. This limestone outcrop is on the largest hill in the El Cayo zone and is opposite the island of El Cayo. The cave's proximity to the "island" (actually connected to the right shore during the dry season) undoubtedly accounts for the high concentration of chipped stone tools and chipping debris found in the cave. The island is built up of tons of small waterworn pebbles of all kinds and colors together with drift sand and is situated at the mouth of a narrow canyon from which the Usumacinta River issues, as described earlier.

High forest rises from the flat valley floor and the steep hillside, masking the front of the cave and shutting out the sunlight so that the cave is quite dark. The mouth of the cave is 15 m wide and 8 m high; the cave is 15 m deep (Fig. 14). From the artifactual and non-artifactual material on the floor of the cave it was obvious that it had been used at various times as a domestic shelter and as a burial site. Although the deposit was not entirely dry or undisturbed, it appeared rather deep and quite promising, particularly near the mouth of the cave. Near the back of the cave, the bedrock slopes up gradually until only bare rock serves as the cave floor. Larger pieces of limestone roof fall tended to close off the back. A small seep was found in the rear of the cave, but in January (1965) it was already beginning to dry up; obviously it was not a permanent water source, but the intermittent seep had considerably dampened the deposit inside the cave. This fact was not apparent or even suggested by sur-

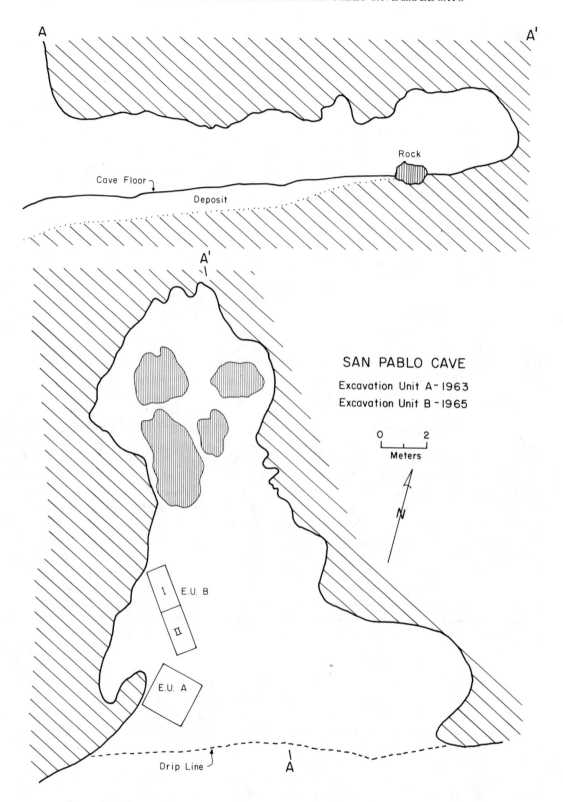

Figure 14.   PLAN AND SECTION OF SAN PABLO CAVE SHOWING LOCATION OF EXCAVATIONS A AND B

face observation; the dry, dusty floor belied completely the sub-surface condition.

The matrix in the cave deposit was a fine, tan, silty sand. It contained large quantities of chipped stone artifacts and debris, human and animal bone, freshwater and marine shell, pottery, and of course, numerous small limestone spalls from the roof of the cave.

Two excavations of different sizes were made in the deposit. Each was controlled by arbitrary 20 cm levels since natural levels were unrecognizable even after excavation, though this may have been due to insufficient light and the damp nature of the lower part of the deposit. Mixing over the years, however, is more probably the reason that the deposit appeared to be rather homogenous from top to bottom. Each excavation is described below.

Excavation Unit A (1963)

This was a small 2 m by 2 m pit dug in four 20 cm levels (San Pablo Cave Samples SPC-A 1–4; Table 1) near the left wall well beyond the drip line (Fig. 14). Considerable concern was exercised in selecting the location of this pit to examine the deposit adequately but not to place it where it might complicate any future excavation. We did not have the equipment to screen the earth from this pit.

Excavation Unit B (1965)

This excavation was laid out as a 1 m by 8 m trench, divided into four equal 2 m sections (Figs. 15, 16). Sections were labeled by Roman numerals in succession from the interior of the cave outward. Excavation of the first two sections (I and II) was by 20 cm levels (SPC-BI 1 through 4; SPC-BII 1 through 4, Table 1) and carried out by buckets to screens where all artifacts and non-artifactual remains were separated from the dirt and then bagged and tagged.

All levels contained a high concentration of bone and shell and a particularly high frequency of chipped stone artifacts. Very small sherds were found in all levels but never in great numbers.

The deposit was considerably wetter than my first estimate indicated and while not so wet as to

have destroyed the bone and shell, there was little hope of finding other more perishable material such as wood, grass, or textiles. The humidity was sufficient to prohibit free passage of the material through a 5 mm screen and so slowed the sifting process that the proposed Sections III and IV were not excavated.

Burials

Four burials were found during the excavation, one of which was in a small rock-lined and capped tomb.

Burial 1 (Fig. 17)
Location: North end of Excavation Unit B-I, Level 2.
Type: Simple grave with rough limestone slabs used as grave floor.
Individuals: One adult (40+ years) and one child (7 years); sex unknown.
Offering: Necklace of 10 tubular stone beads, 6 shell discs, and 2 spherical jade beads (Fig. 18a–c).
Period: Late Classic (?).

Burial 2 (Fig. 17)
Location: Center section of Excavation Unit B-I, Level 2.
Type: Simple grave.
Individuals: Two adults (16+ years), sex unknown, and one male adolescent, (14 years); all in very poor condition.
Offerings: Small, slender jade pendant (Fig. 18d) and nacre bird pendant (Fig. 18e).
Period: Late Classic (?).

Burial 3 (Fig. 19)
Location: Northern half of Excavation Unit B-I, Levels 3 and 4.
Type: Simple grave.
Individuals: Four adults, one extended on right side with face turned up; two males, one female, and one undetermined.
Offering: One partial deer mandible may not be purposeful offering, but part of the burial fill.

Burial 4 (Fig. 20)
Location: North end of Excavation Unit B-II, Levels 1–4.

Figure 15. EXCAVATION UNIT B, SAN PABLO CAVE, WORK IN PROGRESS

Figure 16. EXCAVATION UNIT B, TOMB 2

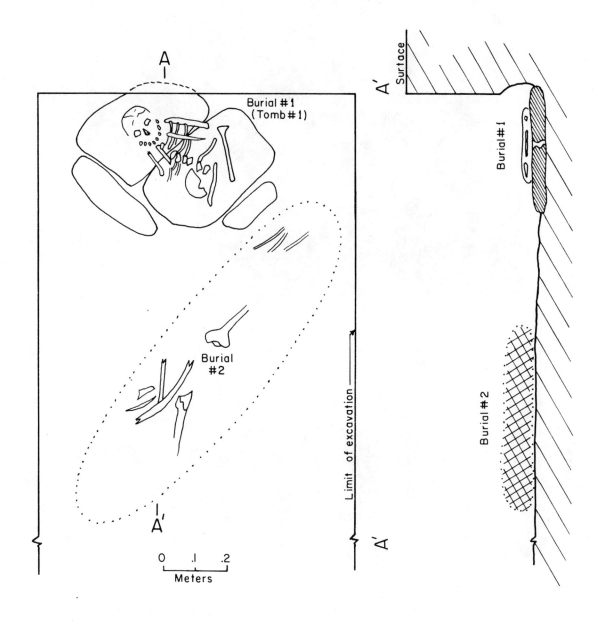

Figure 17.   PLAN AND SECTION OF BURIALS 1 AND 2

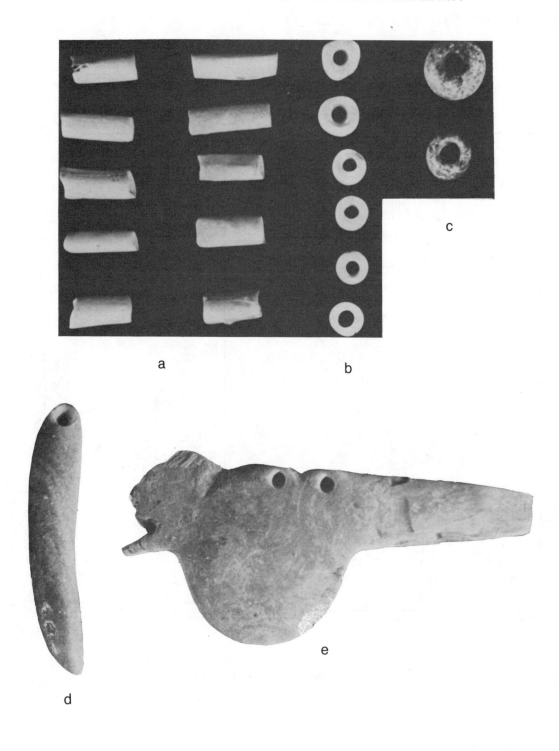

Figure 18.   OFFERINGS OF BURIAL 1 AND BURIAL 2
a. ten tubular beads; *b.* six shell disc beads; *c.* two spherical jade beads; *d.* jade pendant; *e.* bird effigy shell pendant.
Twice natural size.

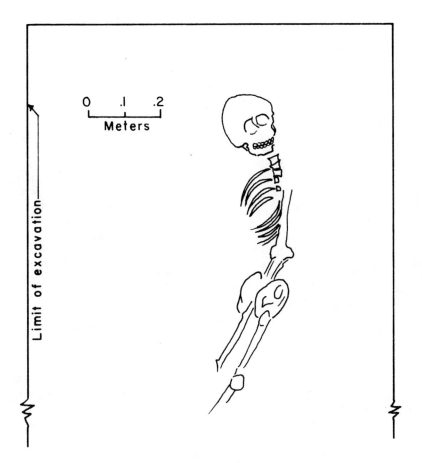

Figure 19. PLAN AND SECTION OF BURIAL 3

Type: Tomb-like chamber excavated 10 cm into bedrock; walls made of limestone slabs placed on end, roof capped with larger limestone slabs; interior dimensions of the tomb: width 42 cm, height 39 cm, and length 71 cm. Labeled Tomb 2 in the field and in Table 1.

Individuals: One adult, associated with offering; two young adults (16+ years), one mature adult in the west end of the tomb; sex undetermined (at least one possible male, at least one possible female).

Offerings:

a) One Pucte Brown: Pucte Variety pedestal jar (Fig. 21*c*); ht. 17.4 cm, rim diam. 14.3 cm, max. body diam. 19.5 cm, wall th. 0.7 cm.

b) Two Pucte Brown: Pucte Variety flaring-rim, basal-flange, hollow-support tripod bowls; whole vessel (Fig. 21*d*), ht. 11 cm, rim diam. 30.3 cm, base diam. 22.5 cm; partial vessel (Fig. 24*b*), ht. about 12 cm, rim diam. 37.1 cm, base diam. 28 cm.

c) Two Aguila Orange: Aguila Variety small, polished, direct-wall bowls with slightly curved bases and red-slipped exteriors (Figs. 21*a*, *b*); both are the same size: ht. 5.6 cm, rim diam. 13.4 cm, base diam. 1.2 cm, wall th. 0.7 cm.

Period: Early Classic, probably Tzakol 2 (A.D. 350–450).

Remarks: The tomb was obviously reused, the latest reuse probably in Tzakol 2 times; artifactual and non-artifactual material not thought to be part of the offering, such as sherds, chipped stone, animal bone, and shell, was designated as tomb fill.

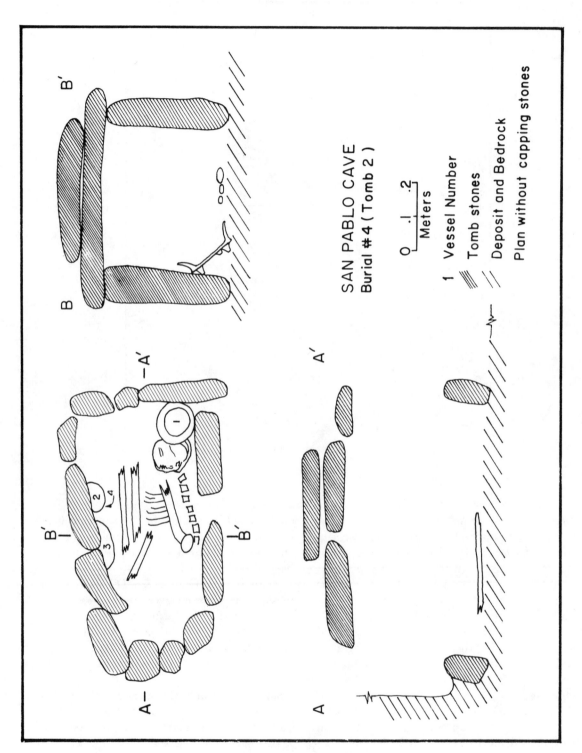

SAN PABLO CAVE
Burial #4 (Tomb 2)

Meters

1   Vessel Number

    Tomb stones

    Deposit and Bedrock

    Plan without capping stones

Figure 20.   PLAN AND SECTION OF BURIAL 4 (TOMB 2)

Figure 21.   BURIAL 4 OFFERING
a, b. Aguila Orange: Aguila Variety bowls; *c*. Pucte Brown: Pucte Variety pedestal jar; *d*. Pucte Brown: Pucte Variety hollow-support tripod bowl. Just less than half size.

DISCUSSION

I estimate that we excavated 3.5 percent of the deposit behind the drip line of the cave. If our more recent experience in testing Central Chiapas shelter-type cave deposits holds true for San Pablo Cave, we can expect that the deposit will be many times greater than that available inside the cave proper if the debris deposited outside the cave in the downslope talus is included. Results of our recent investigations at Camcum Rock Shelter (Lee and Clark 1980), a cave very similar to San Pablo Cave in size, shape, and topographical location, demonstrate that there is a quantum leap upward in quantity and quality of the deposit outside the cave compared to that inside it; not only is there much more material deposited outside the cave in the downslope, but because of its steep decline, it has been much less disturbed than the cave floor itself.

There was no indication of any natural stratigraphy in either of the two excavations in San Pablo Cave; the deposit appeared to be rather homogenous. Undoubtedly this is the result of extensive mixing. There is a typological and stratigraphic difference in the burials.

It is possible that the desirability of this cave as a burial spot over a long period of time (Remnants of 23 individuals were recovered in our small sample!) had led to the almost complete destruction of any natural or cultural stratigraphy once present. The hope is, however, that somewhere, perhaps deeper in the deposit towards the front or in the outside slope, debris was allowed to accumulate and remain undisturbed. The cave merits a more complete and careful excavation. The location of both preliminary excavations was selected to do as little damage as possible to the deposit and with an eye towards a larger, longer, more complete excavation sometime in the future.

CERAMICS OF EL CAYO

The collection of ceramics from El Cayo is small: 1,090 sherds and five whole and partial vessels. About 58 percent of the pottery can be assigned to types and/or varieties already named, described, and published in the Lowland Maya archaeological literature. Therefore, no type and/or variety descriptions are attempted here, nor are formal ceramic complexes set up for El Cayo; ceramics assignable to already established types are listed under those names. All formal type-variety identifications were made by Joseph W. Ball.

The ceramics are from a surface survey made without clearing and from the two small pits excavated to determine the general nature of the cave deposit. We wanted to learn the basic cultural characteristics of the cave, such as chronological extension, cultural relationships, and cave function, as well as the physical properties of the cave deposit such as size, depth, relative dryness, texture, composition, etc., without making a great commitment in time and money. The results of this preliminary testing provide a basis from which to decide if the cave appears to warrant more time and effort, but they do not allow us to use the ceramics or other artifacts for more than the most provisional statements concerning function and temporal/spatial relationships.

In listing the named types and varieties that we found at El Cayo, I have given the original citation to the established type and/or variety, the chronological position, the intersite distribution and ceramic sphere relationship, the size of the sample, intrasite distribution, and remarks. The types and/or varieties are ordered by ceramic horizons, from early to late. The reader is referred to the original description and discussion of Lowland Maya ceramic horizons and spheres in Willey, Culbert, and Adams (1967: 269–315); for the temporal and spatial extent of each sphere see Ball (1976).

Those few sherds which do not fit an established type or variety are described briefly, but no classification is established here. Vessel forms reconstructed from fragmentary sherds are illustrated, as are certain other classes with distinctive surface decoration. Examples of the typed ceramic specimens are also illustrated along with whole or partial vessels.

Color descriptions are from the Munsell Soil Color Charts (Munsell 1954). Hardness is assigned according to the Moh's scale.

The provenience and frequency of ceramics collected in the El Cayo region are given in Table 1 by type and/or variety name or general, descriptive, temporary name. The named types and varieties are given in order from earliest to latest.

ESTABLISHED TYPES/VARIETIES

Mamom Ceramics

Muxanal Red-on-cream: Variety Unspecified (3 sherds; Fig. 22*a*)
Established: Named by Smith and Gifford (1966: 160) based on Smith's (1955) description for Uaxactun.
Chronological position: 600–300 B.C. (Willey, Culbert, and Adams 1967, Fig. 10).
Intersite distribution: Mamom ceramic sphere. A different variety is rare in the San Felipe complex at Altar de Sacrificios (Adams 1971: 27–28). Extensive Lowland Maya distribution is given by Ball (1977: 48).
El Cayo distribution: Highest levels in San Pablo Cave (2 sherds) and surface of Group B (1 sherd).

Chunhinta Black: Chunhinta Variety (40 sherds; Fig. 22*b*)
Established: Named by Smith and Gifford (1966: 156), based on Smith's (1955) description for Uaxactun.
Chronological position: San Felix phase, early facet at Altar de Sacrificios (Adams 1971: 24, Table 26); Escoba phase at Seibal (Sabloff 1975, Fig. 4).
Intersite distribution: Mamom ceramic sphere. Infrequent at Altar de Sacrificios; relatively im-

Table 1. Ceramic Frequencies by Provenience

Provenience	Muxanal Red-on-Cream	Chunhinta Black	Pital Cream	Juventud Red	Aguila Orange	Triunfo Striated	Puele Brown	Dos Arroyos Orange Polychrome	Dos Arroyos Orange Polychrome 1	Dos Arroyos Orange Polychrome 2	Caldero Buff Polychrome	Dos Aguadas Gray Polychrome	Hool Orange Polychrome	Undescribed/unnamed Cream Polychrome	Moro Orange Polychrome	Saxche Orange Polychrome: Saxche	Saxche Orange Polychrome: Acul	Desquite Red-on-Orange	Gua Red-on-Cream	Dzibalche Orange-Buff	Tinaja Red	Trapiche Incised: Trapiche Variety
Group B																						
ECR-1	1					4																
ECR-2						3																
Group C																						
ECR-3		1			2	1							11	4				10			4	
ECR-4			2		2												1			1		
ECR-5				1															3			
ECR-6					1	1																
ECR-7					1	1							2					1			4	1
San Pablo Cave																						
SPC-4					1	3	2															
SPC-F-1963								1			1		1									
Excavation Unit A SPC-A-1		2			6	17	8	1								1						
SPC-A-2		3		1	1	14	3	1				1		1								
SPC-A-3		2			5	10	2		2													
SPC-A-4		2			4	2	6	1														
Excavation Unit B SPC-BI-1	1	10	2		15	20	12	4			1					1						
SPC-BI-2		4		1	2	6	3					1		1		1						
SPC-BI-3		1			3	4		2														
SPC-BI-4		1						1														
SPC-BII-1	1	3	4	1	16	7	10			1		1										
SPC-BII-2		6	14	2	7	9	6								1			1		1		
SPC-BII-3		4	3		8	3	2															
SPC-BII-4																						
SPC-Tomb 2-Fill		1			23	22	6	1			2					2						
TOTAL	3	40	25	6	97	127	60	12	2	1	4	3	14	6	1	5	1	12	3	2	8	1

Table 1. CERAMIC FREQUENCIES BY PROVENIENCE cont.

Provenience		Trapiche Incised: Ixpayac Variety	Cedro Gadrooned	Altar Orange	Provincia Plano-Relief	Carche Incised	Unnamed Plano-Relief	Fine Striated	Coarse Paste, Smoothed	Coarse Paste, Scraped	Thin, Polished Black	Fine Buff Paste	Hard, Slipped White	Coarse Paste, Slipped White	Coarse Red Paste	Tan Paste, Slipped Red	Polished Brown	Unslipped Tan	Appliqued, Crude Paste	Red-on-Orange	TOTAL
Group B	ECR-1								1	5											11
	ECR-2																				3
Group C	ECR-3	5	5	13	1	1										3					45
	ECR-4			3					2			3			1	1	1				31
	ECR-5			1					2							1					7
	ECR-6									3											7
	ECR-7	3		9																	20
San Pablo Cave	SPC-4								2	4	1					1	3				17
	SPC-F-1963																				3
Excavation Unit A	SPC-A-1			1				4	20	14		3									77
	SPC-A-2							15	20	32	1	1				2		1			99
	SPC-A-3							4	11	9	2	2				1					50
	SPC-A-4								3	3						1					23
Excavation unit B	SPC-BI-1			5				19	20	48	9	7			3	3	1	1			182
	SPC-BI-2			1				16	14	10	5	2	1		2	2					72
	SPC-BI-3							5	6	1											21
	SPC-BI-4						1	1	4	2											9
	SPC-BII-1							20	40	29	7	1				2			1	1	145
	SPC-BII-2							24	41	20	3					1	1				137
	SPC-BII-3			1				16	13	13			1		1	3	1	1			69
	SPC-BII-4							3	4	1						2					10
	SPC-Tomb 2-Fill							3	14	10				3	2	2					93
TOTAL		8	5	34	1	1	1	130	217	204	28	19	2	3	9	25	7	3	1	1	1,131

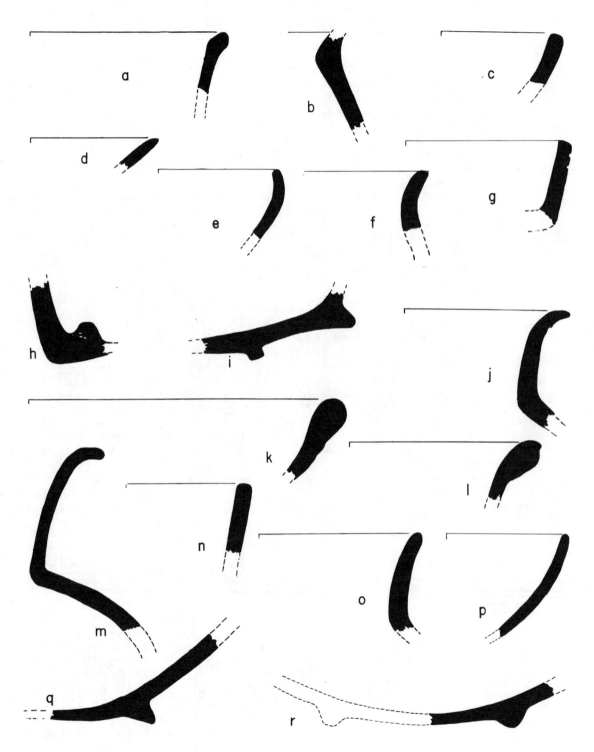

Figure 22.   Ceramics of the Mamom and Tzakol Complexes
a–g. Mamom; *h–r.* Tzakol.
a. Muxanal Red-on-cream; *b.* Chunhinta Black; *c.* Pital Cream; *d–g.* Joventud Red; *h–r.* Aguila Orange. Half size.

portant at Seibal. For intersite description of this and other varieties of the type in the Maya Lowlands see Ball (1977: 30).

El Cayo distribution: Restricted to San Pablo Cave, with highest frecuencies in the upper levels.

Pital Cream: Blotchy Variety (25 sherds; Fig. 22c)

Established: Adams (1971: 25–26).

Chronological position: San Felix phase, early facet, at Altar de Sacrificios (Adams 1971, Table 26).

Distribution: Mamom ceramic sphere. Lowland Maya distribution of this type/variety is given by Ball (1977: 36–37)

El Cayo distribution: Upper levels only in San Pablo Cave.

Remarks: This is the second most common type of the Mamom ceramic horizon in San Pablo Cave.

Joventud Red: Jolote Variety (6 sherds; Fig. 22d–g)

Established: Adams (1971: 20–21).

Chronological position: San Felipe phase at Altar de Sacrificios (Adams 1971, Table 26).

Intersite distribution: Appears to be a variety of Joventud Red found only in the western part of the Mamom ceramic sphere. Excellent Lowland Maya distribution of this type/variety is given by Ball (1977: 17–18).

El Cayo distribution: Upper levels only in San Pablo Cave.

Tzakol Ceramics

Aguila Orange: Aguila Variety (95 sherds and 2 whole vessels; Fig. 23a–k)

Established: Named by Smith and Gifford (1966: 154) based on Smith's (1955) description for Uaxactun.

Chronological position: Tzakol horizon at Uaxactun (Smith and Gifford 1966: 171); Salinas through Ayn phases at Altar de Sacrificios (Adams 1971: 26–27); dated to A.D. 225–550 in the Peten-Belize area by Willey, Culbert, and Adams (1967, Fig. 10).

Intersite distribution: Tzakol ceramic sphere.

Distribution in the Maya Lowlands is given by Ball (1977: 41).

El Cayo distribution: Found in all lots and samples except those from Groups B and C and the fourth, or lowest, levels of Excavation Units B-I and B-II in San Pablo Cave. Two whole vessels are from Burial 4 of the cave.

Remarks: Dating can probably be refined. As Adams (1971: 27) points out, there are probably two varieties, one associated with Tzakol 1 and 2 and the other with Tzakol 3; Aguila Orange at El Cayo is more like the earlier variety, which would reduce its chronological range to A.D. 225–400 (Willey, Culbert, and Adams 1967, Fig. 10).

Triunfo Striated: Triunfo Variety (127 sherds; Figs. 23l, 25b, c)

Established: Named by Smith and Gifford (1966: 163) based on Smith's (1955) description for Uaxactun.

Chronological position: Tzakol horizon at Uaxactun (Willey, Culbert, and Adams 1967, Fig. 10).

Intersite distribution: Tzakol ceramic sphere; plentiful at Seibal (Sabloff 1975: 11–102). Lowland Maya distribution of three varieties of this type is given by Ball (1977: 14).

El Cayo distribution: In all groups and in San Pablo Cave except for three lots, the fourth, or lowest, levels of Excavation Units B-I and B-II and a surface collection made in 1963.

Pucte Brown: Pucte Variety (57 sherds, 1 partial vessel, and 2 whole vessels; Figs. 21c, d; 24a ii; 25a, d, f, h, i)

Established: Named by Smith and Gifford (1966: 161–171) based on Smith's (1955) description for Uaxactun.

Chronological position: Tzakol 2 at Uaxactun (Willey, Culbert, and Adams 1967, Fig. 10); late Ayn phase at Altar de Sacrificios (Adams 1971: 22).

Intersite distribution: Tzakol ceramic sphere. Lowland Maya distribution is given by Ball (1977: 24).

El Cayo distribution: Only in San Pablo Cave, where it was concentrated in the upper levels; it was not found at all in Level 4 of Excavation Unit B. Whole vessels are from Burial 4, the partial vessel from Excavation Unit B-II-1.

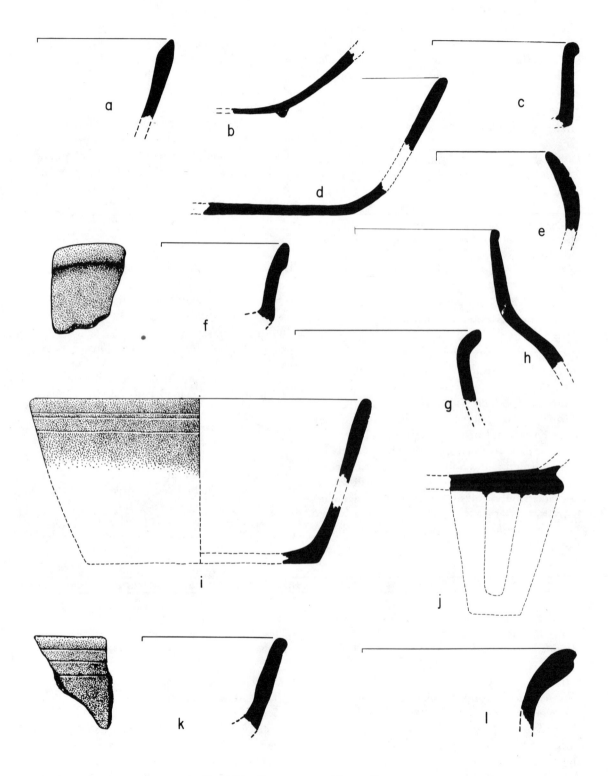

Figure 23.   CERAMICS OF THE TZAKOL COMPLEX
a–k. Aguila Orange; *l*. Triunfo Striated. Half size.

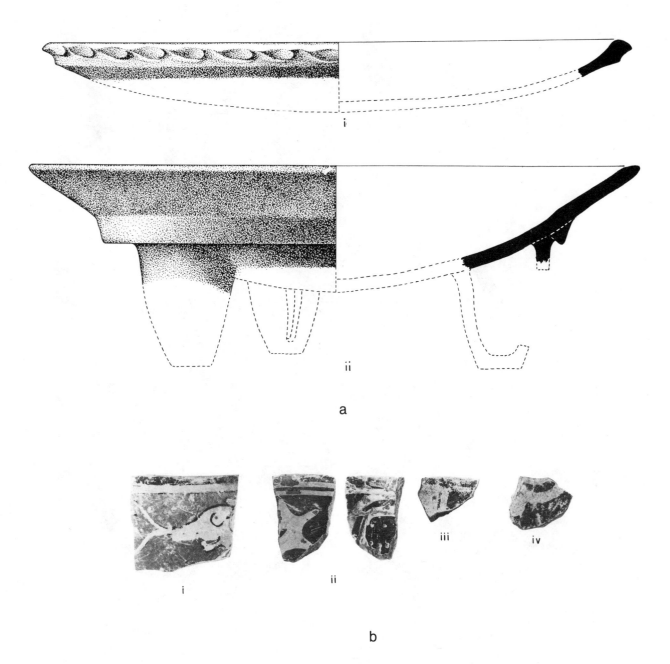

Figure 24. Ceramics of the Tzakol Complex
a,i. Coarse paste, scraped; *a, ii.* Pucte Brown. (Both from Tomb 2, but probably not part of Burial 4 offering.)
b, i. Saxche Orange Polychrome: Acul Variety; *b, ii–iv.* Gua Red-on-cream: Gua Variety. Just less than half size.

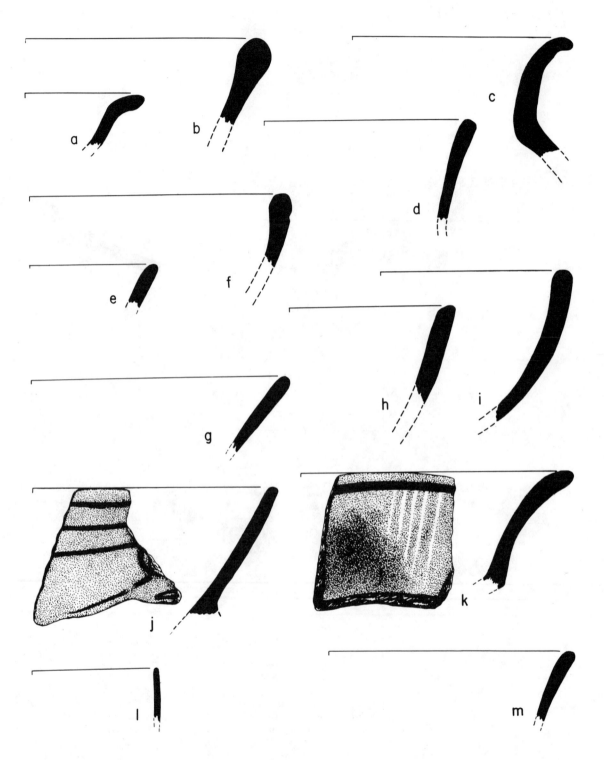

Figure 25.   CERAMICS OF THE TZAKOL COMPLEX

a, d, f, h, i. Pucte Brown; *b, c.* Triunfo Striated; *e, g.* Dos Arroyos Orange Polychrome; *j.* Dos Arroyos Orange Polychrome: Variety Unspecified 1; *k, l.* Dos Arroyos Orange Polychrome: Variety Unspecified 2; *m.* Caldero Buff Polychrome. Half size.

Dos Arroyos Orange Polychrome: Dos Arroyos Variety (12 sherds; Fig. 25e, g)

Established: Named by Smith and Gifford (1966: 157, 171) based on Smith's (1955) description for Uaxactun.

Chronological position: Tzakol 2–3 at Uaxactun; at Altar de Sacrificios an almost identical variety occurs in a more restricted time range, from the Late Ayn phase to the Veremos phase (Adams 1971: 37).

Intersite distribution: Tzakol ceramic sphere. Unspecified varieties are present at Seibal (Sabloff 1975: 105, 106) where the pottery is highly eroded. The distribution of this variety in the Maya Lowlands and Highlands is given by Ball (1977: 67, 68).

El Cayo distribution: Only in San Pablo Cave lots where it was limited to the upper levels except for 1 sherd in Excavation Unit A, Level 4.

Remarks: The presence of a sherd of this type in Level 4 of Excavation Unit A suggests that the edges of the cave deposit are more mixed than the center.

Dos Arroyos Orange Polychrome: Variety Unspecified 1 (2 sherds; Fig. 25j)

Established: See Dos Arroyos Variety, above.

Chronological position: See Dos Arroyos Variety, above.

Intersite distribution: Tzakol ceramic sphere. The distribution of related varieties of the same type in both the Maya Lowlands and Highlands is given by Ball (1977: 67, 68).

El Cayo distribution: Only in tomb fill of Burial 4, San Pablo Cave.

Dos Arroyos Orange Polychrome: Variety Unspecified 2 (1 sherd; Fig. 25k, l)

Established: See Dos Arroyos Variety, above.

Chronological position: See Dos Arroyos Variety, above.

Intersite distribution: Tzakol ceramic sphere. The distribution of related varieties of this type in the Maya Lowlands and Highlands is given by Ball (1977: 67, 68).

El Cayo distribution: Found in tomb fill of Burial 4, San Pablo Cave.

Caldero Buff Polychrome: Caldero Variety (4 sherds; Figs. 25m, 26a)

Established: Named by Smith and Gifford (1966: 155) based on description of Uaxactun ceramics by Smith (1955).

Chronological position: Tzakol 2–3 (Willey, Culbert, and Adams 1967, Fig. 10); at Altar de Sacrificios Adams (1971: 37) dates it to the Late Ayn phase.

Intersite distribution: Tzakol ceramic sphere. Known distribution in the Maya Lowlands includes Uaxactun (Smith 1955) and Barton Ramie (unspecified variety; Gifford 1976: 179, 180).

El Cayo distribution: On the surface and in one upper level in San Pablo Cave.

Dos Aguadas Gray Polychrome: Dos Aguadas Variety (3 sherds; Fig. 26b)

Established: Named by Smith and Gifford (1966: 157), based on Smith's (1955) description for Uaxactun.

Chronological position: Tzakol 3 (Willey, Culbert, and Adams 1967, Fig. 10).

Intersite distribution: Tzakol ceramic sphere. Distribution includes Becan (Ball 1977: 77) and Uaxactun (Smith 1955, Figs. 34a7, 9).

El Cayo distribution: Second levels of the adjacent excavation units in San Pablo Cave.

Tepeu 1–2 Ceramics

Hool Orange Polychrome: Variety Unspecified (14 sherds; Fig. 26c, d)

Established: Not established.

Chronological position: A.D. 580–740 (Ball and Andrews 1975: 233).

Intersite distribution: At Dzibilchaltun Ball says it is probably of Chenes origin (Ball and Andrews 1975: 233). A whole vessel of this class has been identified by Ball (personal communication, June 1975) in the reconnaissance collections from the Upper Grijalva River Basin, Site Tr-76 (Lee 1979, Fig. 2).

El Cayo distribution: From floor and Level 1 of San Pablo Cave and from the interior of Temple 3, the center temple of Maler's Temple of the Five Temples.

Undescribed Cream Polychrome (6 sherds; Fig. 26e)

Established: Not established.

Chronological position: Tepeu 2.

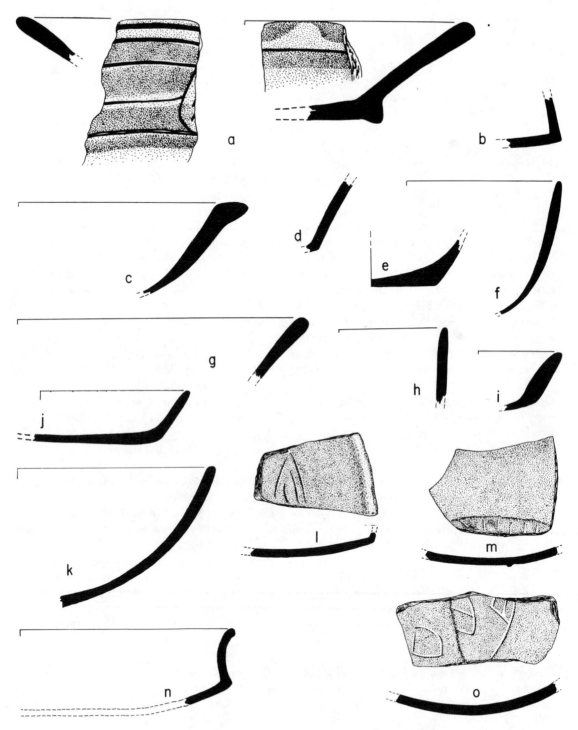

Figure 26.   CERAMICS OF THE TZAKOL, TEPEU 1–2, AND TEPEU 3 COMPLEXES
a, *b*. Tzakol; *c–i*. Tepeu 1 and 2; *h–o*. Tepeu 3.
a. Caldero Buff Polychrome; *b*. Dos Aguadas Gray Polychrome; *c*, *d*. Hool Orange Polychrome; *e*. Undescribed Cream
Polychrome; *f*. Moro Orange Polychrome; *g*. Saxche Orange Polychrome; *h*. Desquite Red-on-orange; *i*. Dzibalche
Orange-buff; *j*, *k*. Tinaja Red; *n*. Trapiche Incised: Trapiche Variety; *l*, *m*, *o*. Trapiche Incised: Decorated Interior
(Ixpayac) Variety. Half size.

Intersite distribution: Unknown.

El Cayo distribution: San Pablo Cave.

Remarks: Appears to be a Tepeu 2 equivalent of Hool Orange Polychrome.

Moro Orange Polychrome: Variety Unspecified (1 sherd; Fig. 26*f*)

Established: Ball (1973: 144).

Chronological position: Bejuco ceramic complex (A.D. 600–700; Ball 1973, Table 1) at Becan (Ball and Andrews 1975: 232).

Intersite distribution: Rio Bec-Chenes origin; varieties present at Becan, Dzibilchaltun, and Uaxactun (rare).

El Cayo distribution: San Pablo Cave, fill of Burial 4.

Remarks: Not the Rio Bec variety, as the designs are different.

Saxche Orange Polychrome: Saxche Variety (5 sherds; Fig. 26*g*)

Established: Named by Smith and Gifford (1966: 162) based on the description by Smith (1955) for Uaxactun.

Chronological position: Tepeu 1 at Uaxactun (Willey, Culbert, and Adams 1967, Fig. 10), Chixoy and Early Pasion at Altar de Sacrificios (Adams 1971: 38).

Intersite distribution: Tepeu 1 ceramic sphere. Ball and Andrews (1975: 232) report it as common in north central Peten, southwestern Campeche, and southwestern Quintana Roo. The Lowland Maya distribution of this and other varieties of this type is given by Ball (1977: 68, 71, 72).

El Cayo distribution: San Pablo Cave, from the first level of the excavations (2 sherds), from the lowest (fourth) level (1 sherd), and from the fill of Burial 4 (2 sherds).

Saxche Orange Polychrome: Acul Variety (1 sherd; Fig. 24*b* i)

Established: Adams (1971: 37) at Altar de Sacrificios.

Chronological position: Veremos and Chixoy ceramic complexes.

Intersite distribution: This type is only known at Altar de Sacrificios and El Cayo.

El Cayo distribution: Surface of Group C, Structure 3 (ECR–4; Table 1).

Remarks: This type is probably present at other sites along the Usumacinta River between Altar de Sacrificios and El Cayo with occupations of the same period.

Desquite Red-on-orange: Desquite Variety (12 sherds; Fig. 26*h*)

Established: Smith and Gifford (1966: 157), based on description by Smith (1955) for Uaxactun.

Chronological position: Tepeu 1 at Uaxactun (Willey, Culbert, and Adams 1967, Fig. 10).

Intersite distribution: Tepeu 1 ceramic sphere. Reported only from Uaxactun.

El Cayo distribution: Pothunters' back dirt at the front of the Temple of the Five Temples (11 sherds) and from Level 2, a middle level, in San Pablo Cave (1).

Gua Red-on-cream: Gua Variety (3 sherds; Fig. 24*b* ii–iv)

Established: Adams (1971: 29, Fig. 35*a*).

Chronological position: Veremos ceramic complex (Adams 1977: 29, Table 26) at Altar de Sacrificios.

El Cayo distribution: All from surface of Group C, Structure S (ECR-5; Table 1).

Remarks: Adams relates this type to San Bartolo Red-on-buff at Uaxactun, but it appears to me to be closer to Naranjal Red-on-cream at the same site. At El Cayo it sometimes has decoration on the interior and the designs are bolder, not as finely painted as those at Altar de Sacrificios. Similar to Naranjal Red-on-cream at Uaxactun (Smith and Gifford 1966: 160; Smith 1955, Vol. 1, pp. 171, 175, 176; Vol. 2, Figs. 34*c*9, 58*b*3, 60*a*3, 64*a*4, 74*a*).

Dzibalche Orange Buff: Dzibalche Variety (2 sherds; Fig. 26*i*)

Chronological position: Bejuco ceramic complex at Becan (Ball 1977: 133, Table 1).

Intersite distribution: Jaina, Piedras Negras, Guaymil, Becan, and at Chicanna in Campeche and perhaps at Trinidad, Tabasco (Ball 1977: 42, 45).

El Cayo distribution: Level 3, a middle level, of Excavation Unit B I in San Pablo Cave.

Remarks: Ball (1977: 45) explains his separation of this Becan type/variety from his previously described Dzibilchaltun Orange (Ball 1973: 88–89) which has a more northern distribution.

Tepeu 3 Ceramics

Tinaja Red: Tinaja Variety (8 sherds; Fig. 26*j*, *k*)
Established: Smith and Gifford (1966: 163), based on description by Smith (1955) for Uaxactun.
Chronological position: Tepeu 3 at Uaxactun (Willey, Culbert, and Adams 1967: Fig. 10), Boca phase at Altar de Sacrificios (Adams 1971: 23); present at Seibal, but the situation is unclear as the type appears to begin as early as the Tepejilote phase and lasts until the end of the Bayal phase (Sabloff 1975: 158–160, Fig. 4).
Intersite distribution: Probably Tepeu and Boca ceramic spheres (Willey, Culbert, and Adams 1967: 310, 311; Adams 1971: 23; Sabloff 1975: 158). Distribution in the Maya Lowlands includes Uaxactun, Altar de Sacrificios, and Seibal; two other varieties of the type are also present at Altar de Sacrificios (Adams 1971: 23).
El Cayo distribution: Pothunters' back dirt on Temple of the Five Temples.
Remarks: Common at Becan (Ball 1977: 23), which may suggest that the northern limits of the Tepeu ceramic sphere should be extended farther northward.

Trapiche Incised: Trapiche Variety (1 sherd; Fig. 26*n*)
Established: Smith and Gifford (1966: 163–173); known earlier as part of Y Fine Orange (Smith 1958, Fig. 2); better descriptions by Adams (1971: 45) and Sabloff (1970: 374, 377; 1975: 192, 194).
Chronological position: Tepeu 3 at Uaxactun (Willey, Culbert, and Adams 1967, Fig. 10), Late Boca and Jimba phases at Seibal (Sabloff 1970: 374; Willey 1970, Fig. 2).
Intersite distribution: Not known; it appears to be limited to ". . . an area roughly limited by southeastern Chiapas, eastern Tabasco, southern Campeche, western British Honduras, and the Alta Verapaz of Guatemala . . ." (Smith 1958: 151, 153). Lowland Maya distribution includes only the three above-mentioned sites as well as Becan (Ball 1977: 88) and Marquez Collection (Sabloff 1975: 194).

El Cayo distribution: Group C only; pothunters' backdirt on the river side of Temple 5 of the Temple of the Five Temples at about the level of the interior plaza floor.

Trapiche Incised: Decorated Interior (Ixpayac) Variety (8 sherds; Fig. 26*l*, *m*, *o*)
Established: Adams (1971: 45); more completely described by Sabloff (1975: 194, 195).
Chronological position: Jimba phase at Altar de Sacrificios, where it was given the name Ixpayac (Adams 1971, Table 26).
Intersite distribution: Boca ceramic sphere; present in the Bayal ceramic complex at Seibal (Sabloff 1970, Figs. 53, 54*g*; 1975: 194, 195), the Jimba ceramic complex at Altar de Sacrificios, and is also known from Poptun collection (Adams 1971: 45).
El Cayo distribution: Group C, in the pothunters' backdirt from plaza floor in front of the Temple of the Five Temples.
Remarks: Name changed from Ixpayac to Decorated Interior by Sabloff (1975: 194) to agree with conventions established at the 1965 conference on the Ceramics of the Maya Lowlands (Willey, Culbert and Adams 1967); the variety was not originally recognized from Seibal by Sabloff (1975: 194).

Cedro Gadrooned: Cedro Variety (5 sherds; Fig. 27*d*)
Established: Smith and Gifford (1966: 156); known earlier as part of Y Fine Orange (Smith 1958: 151, 153, Fig. 2); better descriptions by Adams (1971: 46, 47) and Sabloff (1970: 377, 381; 1975: 204).
Chronological position: Tepeu 3 ceramic complex at Uaxactun (Willey, Culbert, and Adams 1967, Fig. 10); Jimba ceramic complex at Altar de Sacrificios (Adams 1971: 46, 47); Late Bayal complex at Seibal (Sabloff 1970: 377-381).
Intersite distribution: Same distribution as Trapiche Incised: Trapiche Variety, above.
El Cayo distribution: Group C, plaza floor in front of the Temple of the Five Temples in pothunters' backdirt.
Remarks: Part of the Fine Orange development.

Altar Orange: Altar Variety (34 sherds; Fig. 27*a–c*, *e–g*, *i*)

Established: Smith and Gifford (1966: 173), based on earlier description of Y Fine Orange (Smith 1958, Fig. 2); more complete description by Sabloff (1975: 189, 192).

Chronological position: Jimba phase complex at Altar de Sacrificios (Adams 1971: 27); slightly earlier Late Bayal phase at Seibal (Sabloff 1970: 362; Willey 1970, Fig. 2).

Intersite distribution: Altar de Sacrificios, Seibal, Yaxchilan, eastern Tabasco Lowlands (Berlin 1956: Fig. 3a, cc, dd, mm–vv; Smith 1958) and Becan (Ball 1977: 45–47).

El Cayo distribution: Inside temple room of Structure 1 at upper plaza level in Group C; also in upper levels of San Pablo Cave.

Remarks: Part of the Fine Orange Ware development; known earlier as Y Fine Orange (Smith 1958: Fig. 2). Ball (1977: 45–47) has discussed its distribution and the typological problems in defining pottery from the Balancun-Altar-Siho ceramic groups; he suggests that the present subdivisions are artificial.

Provincia Plano-relief: Provincia Variety (1 sherd; Fig. 27h)

Established: Smith and Gifford (1966: 173), based on earlier description of Z Fine Orange (Smith 1958, Fig. 1); better descriptions by Adams (1971: 52) and Sabloff (1975: 208, 209).

Chronological position: Late Classic-Early Postclassic Jimba phase at Altar de Sacrificios (Adams 1971: 52, Table 26); slightly earlier Late Bayal phase at Seibal (Sabloff 1970: 374, 377; Willey 1970, Fig. 2).

Intersite distribution: Seibal, Altar de Sacrificios, and Yaxchilan; rare at Uaxactun (Smith 1955: Fig. 86a), eastern Tabasco Lowlands (Smith 1958), Becan, and Hormiguero (Ball 1977: 101, 102).

El Cayo distribution: Corbel-vaulted room of temple nearest river on top of Structure 1, Group C.

Remarks: Part of the ceramic type known as Z Fine Orange (Smith 1958).

Caribe Incised: Caribe Variety (1 sherd; Fig. 27k)

Established: Smith and Gifford (1966: 173); formerly part of Z Fine Orange (Smith 1958: 151, Fig. 1).

Chronological position: Tepeu 3 at Uaxactun (Smith 1955; Willey, Culbert, and Adams 1967, Fig. 10).

Intersite distribution: Same as that of Provincia Plano-relief: Provincia Variety, above; very rare at Seibal (Sabloff 1975: 218).

El Cayo distribution: Group C, in room nearest the river in the Temple of the Five Temples (Structure 1).

Unassigned Types

Unnamed Plano-relief (1 sherd; Fig. 27j)

Fine orange (2.5YR 6/6) paste with very fine, round, white particles and small, round, red, ferric particles. The exterior is slipped a dark brown (2.5YR 2/2) and well polished. The rim is flat and exteriorly thickened to bolster the rim. A small squarish human head glyph is executed in plano-relief on the exterior just below the rim and probably was part of a rim-band made up of similar elements. The glyph is somewhat like Thompson's (1962: 312) Glyph 731, which occurs in the Paris, Madrid, and Dresden codices. It is significant that this glyphic relationship is found to occur within the group of ceramics which is the latest found at the site, the period just prior to the supposed date of the codices.

Fine Striated (130 sherds; Fig. 27l, m, o)

A relatively hard (Moh's 2–3) dark buff-colored (5YR 7/2) paste with water-worn sand grains and smoothly rounded, very small, dark red ferric nodules. The interior is well smoothed, the exterior striated by a brush perhaps made of grass; striations often cross each other. Jar rims and necks tend to be striated parallel to the vessel rim on the interior and the exterior. The most common form is the jar, but some bowls occur.

Coarse Paste, Smoothed (217 sherds; Figs. 27n, 28a, b, d)

The buff (5YR 7/2) paste of this class is finely textured, but is tempered with 0.5 mm white quartz particles and larger, soft, brown, rounded fragments. Vessel wall thickness may vary from 0.5 to 1.5 cm and may be either soft (Moh's 1) or hard (Moh's 5–6). The exterior is always well smoothed; temper often shows through on the surfaces from the smoothing process. Often the

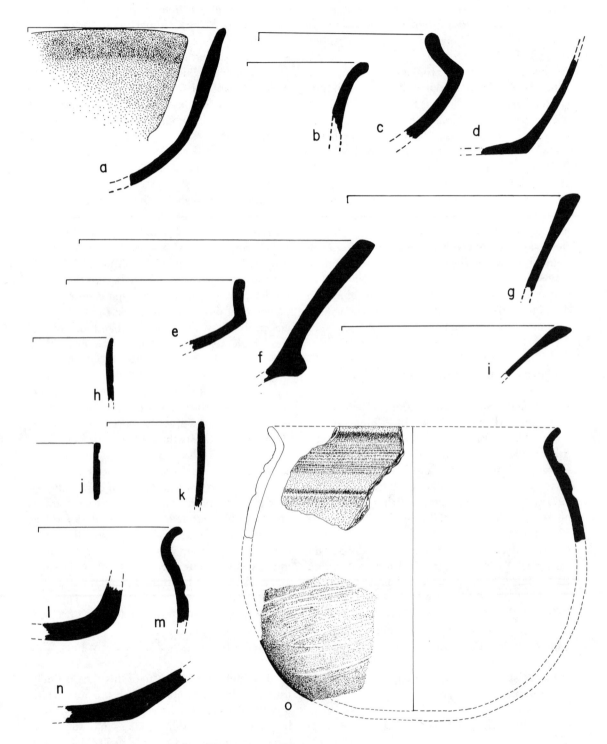

Figure 27.   CERAMICS OF THE TEPEU 3 COMPLEX AND UNASSIGNED TYPES
a–i, k. Tepeu 3; *j, l–o.* other assigned complexes.
a–c, e–g, i. Altar Orange; *d.* Cedro Gadrooned; *h.* Provincia Plano-relief; *j.* Unnamed Plano-relief; *k.* Caribe Incised;
l, m, o. Fine Striated; *n.* Coarse Paste, Smoothed. Half size.

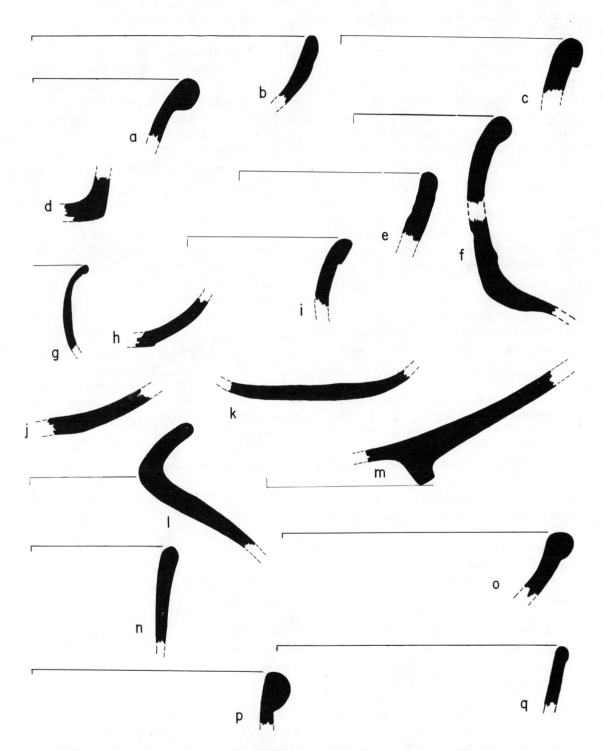

Figure 28. CERAMICS OF UNASSIGNED COMPLEXES
a, b, d. Coarse Paste, Smoothed; c, e, f, i. Coarse Paste, Scraped; g. Fine Buff Paste; h, j. Hard, Slipped White;
k. Coarse Paste, Slipped White. l, m. Coarse Red Paste; n–q. Tan Paste, Slipped Red. Half size.

interior is also well smoothed, but usually less than the exterior. Forms include flat-bottom bowls.

Coarse Paste, Scraped (204 sherds; Figs. 24a i, 28c, e, f, i)

A reddish buff (5YR 7/2) paste is tempered with water-worn sand or crushed calcite. Neither exterior nor interior has been smoothed, but is simply scraped; temper fragments often protrude through the surface and some irregular striation marks occur as the pebble smoother dragged temper particles along the surface during the finishing process. Crushed calcite temper is generally larger than the water-worn sand, but there is less temper in vessels with the former than the latter. Forms include jars.

Thin, Polished Black (28 sherds)

None are distinctive as to form. Most are about 4 mm thick and all have a highly polished exterior with the interior just smoothed or in a few cases, scraped. They are a dark, brownish black (5YR 2/2); the paste hardness is Moh's 2–4. Temper varies from very fine, white particles to somewhat coarser but still finely ground calcite.

Fine Buff Paste (19 sherds; Fig. 28g)

This unslipped buff (5YR 8/2) paste class varies in temper characteristics from none visible with the aid of a 25x hand lens to abundant, fine, sand grains. Paste hardness is Moh's 2–3. Half have sand grain temper and the rest have a combination of finely crushed calcite and small, round, dark red ferric nodules as inclusions. No forms can be reconstructed from the small sample.

Hard, Slipped White (2 sherds; Fig. 28h, j)

These have a thick, creamy white (10YR 8/2) slip on the exterior that has been polished until it has a high sheen. The interior is black (10YR 4/1) to gray (10YR 7/1) and is also very well polished. The paste has a medium texture with abundant, finely-ground, unidentified crystalline temper. Paste hardness is Moh's 5–6. Vessel wall thickness varies from 0.8 cm to 1.1 cm. Form is probably a flat-bottomed bowl with outsloping sides.

Coarse Paste, Slipped White (3 sherds; Fig. 28k)

This paste class is tempered with abundant fine sand grains and very small unidentified particles. The paste is soft (Moh's 2) and friable and contains an occasional small round brown ferric nodule and considerable biotite mica. The paste color ranges from light red (7.5R 6/6) to gray (7.5R 6/0). The exterior surface is covered with a thick, creamy-colored, white fugitive slip which was well-polished, but is now very soft and lusterless. Forms include flat-bottom bowls and small collared jars.

Coarse Red Paste (9 sherds; Figs. 28l, m, 29h)

The heavily tempered paste varies from pink (7.5YR 6/4) to reddish-brown (2.5YR 6/4). Inclusions are sand and very coarsely ground calcite fragments. The bowls are always smoothed on the interior, but only infrequently on the exterior. More often the bowl exteriors are finished only by scraping. The jar is smoothed on the exterior only. Forms include ring-based bowls, flat-bottom bowls with vertical walls and exteriorly everted rounded rim, outflaring-neck jars with round everted rims, and a zoomorphic ladle-handle incense burner (effigy is probably a crocodile).

Tan Paste, Slipped Red (25 sherds; Fig. 28n–q, 29a)

This soft light buff (10YR 8/3) paste group is tempered with crushed calcite, fine white, unidentified, non-crystalline grains, and round ferric nodules. The slip is thick red (2.5YR 5/8), which under certain firing conditions tends to turn brown (7.5R 2.5/4). About half of the vessels are slipped on only one surface, bowls always on the interior and sometimes on the exterior, but jars only on the exterior. A few bowls with only interior slipping have a rough unslipped and unsmoothed exterior. Medium polishing is present. Vessel wall thickness varies from 5 to 12 mm. Vessel forms are cylinders, bolstered rim basins, vertical-walled flat-bottom bowls, and vertical-neck jars with beveled rims. Decoration consists of broad horizontal-line grooving on bowls and jar rims and fine horizontal and diagonal incision on cylinders.

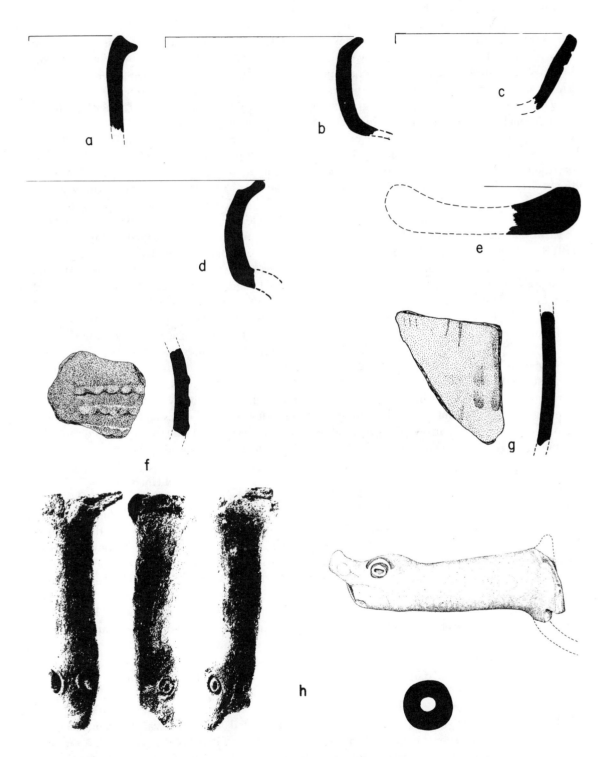

Figure 29.   CERAMICS OF UNASSIGNED COMPLEXES
a. Tan Paste, Slipped Red; *b–d*. Polished Brown; *e*. Unslipped Tan; *f*. Appliqued, Crude Paste; *g*. Red-on-orange; *h*. Coarse Red Paste.

Polished Brown (7 sherds; Fig. 29b–d)

This finely tempered buff (10YR 8/4) to gray (10YR 6/1) colored paste is very hard and takes a high polish. All fragments known have a thin brown (10YR 5/3) slip and have an excellent polish on at least one surface. Temper consists of very fine crystaline and opaque white grains and an occasional round brown ferric nodule. Vessel walls are 2–6 mm thick. Forms include outslanting rims with a rounded lip. Decoration consists of parallel broad-line grooving on the exterior of the bowls just below the rim.

Unslipped Tan (3 sherds; Fig. 29e)

This fine paste ware varies in color from tan (10YR 6/3) to orange (2.5YR 6/8). Fine round ferric nodules and very fine sand temper are present. Vessel wall thickness varies from 3 to 15 mm. Specific vessel form is unknown except for a strangely-shaped incense ladle-handle and incense burner fragments.

Appliqued, Crude Paste (1 sherd; Fig. 29f)

A single thick black sherd, neither slipped nor smoothed, has a series of appliqued narrow fillets on one side. The fillets have finger impressions alternating with narrow peaks to create a serrated effect. Form unknown, but probably part of an incense burner. Wall thickness is 7 mm.

Red-on-orange (1 sherd; Fig. 29g)

Thick paste with wide carbon streak tempered with various-sized, round, red ferric nodules and rare, white, opaque grains. Both exterior and interior are highly polished but unslipped. Wall thickness is 8 mm. Decoration occurs in the form of broad parallel red (7.5R 5/6) lines on one surface, probably a bowl interior.

DISCUSSION OF THE CERAMIC SEQUENCE

The ceramic collection from El Cayo is small and is not considered to be a representative sample from all of El Cayo; for this reason I have not used the term "ceramic complex." Below, in chronological order, is a brief discussion of the ceramics of each horizon.

Mamom Horizon

The earliest ceramics from San Pablo Cave are four types (Muxanal Red-on-cream, Chunhinta Black, Pital Cream, and Joventud Red) of the Mamom ceramic horizon (600–300 B.C.; Table 1). With the exception of 2 sherds found on the surface of Groups B and C, all sherds of this period were found in San Pablo Cave. Only one type, Chunhinta Black, had a general distribution in almost all cave proveniences. The other three types were found almost entirely in the upper levels of the excavations and on the cave floor, clearly demonstrating the disturbed and mixed nature of the deposit within the cave.

The original list of six characteristic types and modes of the Mamom ceramic horizon (Willey, Culbert, and Adams 1967: 307) are represented by only one type at San Pablo Cave, Muxanal Red-on-cream. The other three types are assigned to this horizon at San Pablo on the basis of a similar assessment at Altar de Sacrificios, Seibal, and Uaxactun by the respective authors of more recent reports. The presence of Joventud Red: Jolote Variety at both San Pablo Cave and Altar de Sacrificios suggests that this variety may be typical of the western sector of the Mamom ceramic sphere.

Chicanel Horizon

There were no ceramics in the present El Cayo sample that can be assigned to the Chicanel horizon (300 B.C.–A.D. 225). In spite of the fact that three subdivisions of this horizon were originally defined for the Maya Lowlands, it is a time period not equally represented in all areas. In many parts of Chiapas it is a time of low population, movement of peoples, and highly varied regional ceramic developments.

Tzakol Horizon

There are eight named type/varieties at El Cayo that date to the Tzakol ceramic horizon (A.D. 225–525). All of the polychrome varieties come from San Pablo Cave only. Aguila Orange and Triunfo Striated, two simpler types, occur in almost all proveniences at El Cayo.

The Tzakol ceramic horizon is the most strongly represented of all horizons in the El Cayo zone. It is represented by more named types and more than four times as many individual sherds as the next most important horizon, Mamom (Table 1). This certainly speaks strongly for the local importance of San Pablo Cave, where most ceramics found dated to the Early Classic period.

Several of the type/mode characteristics of the original Tzakol horizon definition are present in the zone (Willey, Culbert, and Adams 1967: 306). It appears to be more significant that none of the several attributes of this horizon which find their origin in the contemporary ceramic complexes at Teotihuacan are present. Is this the reflection of a small community to one side of the mainstream of developments which made themselves felt ceremonially only at larger central places such as Altar de Sacrificios and Uaxactun? Certainly the El Cayo region is well within the spatial limits now known for the Tzakol ceramic sphere, and what affected the sphere generally should be seen at El Cayo, albeit in a weaker version.

Tepeu 1–2 Horizon

This horizon is represented at El Cayo by six Middle–Late Classic (A.D. 525–825) pottery classes. None of the named ceramic varieties appears to date to later than A.D. 700, however. With the exception of the Mamom ceramic horizon, this is the weakest horizon represented at El Cayo, both in numbers of varieties and in total frecuencies (the Mamom ceramic horizon is represented by two fewer varieties but many more individual sherds). The Tepeu 1–2 horizon, like the earlier Tzakol horizon, continued to be characterized by a predominance of polychrome ceramics. Two bichromes make up the other variety of this horizon at El Cayo. With the exception

of two sherds of Hool Polychrome from Group C at El Cayo, the other polychrome sherds all came from San Pablo Cave. Saxche Orange Polychrome is the only named type from the original horizon marker list which was found at El Cayo. It is restricted to Tepeu 1 (Willey, Culbert, and Adams 1967: 306). The other horizon markers from the original list defined by Willey, Culbert, and Adams (1967: 306) that were present at El Cayo include figure-painted polychrome, glyphband polychrome, the flat-based cylinder, and possible polychrome tripod plates—all said to be traits typical of the Tepeu 2 phase. Flat-based cylinders are also found in the Tepeu 3 horizon, but here they are found in Tepeu 2 polychrome types (Hool Orange and Desquite Red-onorange Polychrome).

Tepeu 3 Horizon

This horizon is weakly represented in the El Cayo region by only seven monochrome and various modeled and incised potsherds, all of which appear to date to A.D. 825–950. There are no polychrome types which I can date to this horizon.

Three of the pottery types on the Tepeu 3 horizon list (Willey, Culbert, and Adams 1967: 306) occur at El Cayo. They are Cedro Gadrooned, Trapiche Incised: Trapiche Variety, and Trapiche Incised: Interior Decorated Variety. Only eight sherds of the named types from this horizon were found in San Pablo Cave and all of these except one came from the first two (or latest) levels of the excavations. All other sherds of this horizon came from pothunters' backdirt on Structure 1. Among the unestablished types of pottery, the Tan Paste, Red-slipped class would appear to be of the Tepeu 3 horizon because of its usual appearance with the types usually assigned to this horizon.

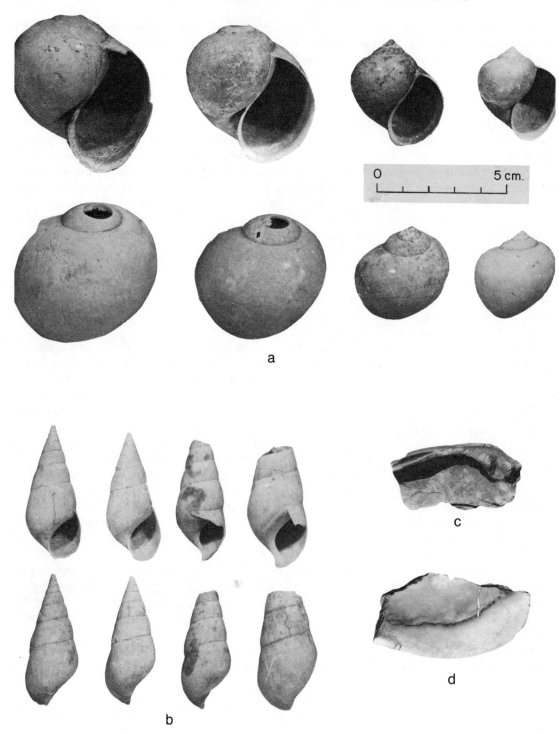

Figure 30.   SNAIL AND CLAM SHELLS
a. land snails; *b*. freshwater snails, all *Pachychilus* cf. *largillierti; c. Psoronaias* cf. *semigranous;*
d. freshwater clam shell fragment.

MISCELLANEOUS ARTIFACTS

STONE

Most artifacts found at San Pablo Cave and El Cayo were either ceramic sherds (Chapter 3) or pieces of chipped stone (Chapter 5). The few artifacts of polished stone, carved bone or shell, and stucco found in our excavations or surface collections are briefly described here.

Stone Beads and Pendant

One spherical jade bead with a biconical hole in the center; diam. 1.4 cm, hole diam. 5 mm.

One spherical jade bead with biconical hole in the center; diam. 1.0 cm; hole diam. 4.5 mm. Part of necklace found with Burial 1 (Fig. 18c).

One tubular jade bead found on the cave floor; diam. .75 cm, length 1.0 cm, hole diam. 3 mm.

Ten slender, tubular, white travertine beads with biconical drilled holes (Fig. 18a); length 1.35–2.0 cm, diam. 0.5–0.7 cm, hole diam. 3.5–4 mm. Part of necklace found with Burial 1.

Small, slender, peg-shaped jade pendant with single biconical hole drilled in one end (Fig. 18d); length 3.6 cm, diam. 0.7 cm; hole diam. 1.5 mm. Found with Burial 2.

SHELL

Shell Ornaments

Mother-of-pearl pendant (Fig. 18e) in the shape of a round-bellied bird. The upper beak, the front of the head, and the end of the tail are missing. Two parallel suspension holes (diam. 1.5 mm) are drilled into the back. Length 5.6 cm, width 2.4 cm, thickness 3 mm. Part of Burial 2.

Six circular disc beads were found with Burial 1 (Fig. 18b). Diam. 0.75–1.0 cm, thick. 2–3 cm, hole diam. 0.3–0.4 cm. Part of necklace offering of Burial 1.

One circular disc bead found on the cave floor. Diam. 0.75 cm, thick. 0.2 cm, hole diam. 3 mm.

Altered and Unaltered Shell

In Table 2 is listed the distribution of altered and unaltered snail and clam shells recovered from the San Pablo Cave excavations. Only some of the snail shells have the tip broken off. It may be assumed fairly safely, on the basis of present and past human use of shellfish in Chiapas, that all freshwater specimens were brought into the cave for consumption (Fig. 30).

The presence of the land snail (Fig. 30a) in the cave is not surprising since it is associated with swidden disturbance of the natural vegetation. This type of agriculture is still practiced in the immediate area.

Table 2. FREQUENCIES OF UNWORKED SHELL BY PROVENIENCE

Provenience	Fresh Water Snail *1	Fresh Water Clam	Fresh Water and Land Snail *2
Ex. A-5-1	1	2	2 *3
5-2	2	3	2
5-3	2	1	2
5-4	1	1	2
Group C		2	
Ex. B-I-1	28	2 *4	2 *3
-2	62	8	16
-3	39	2	11
-4		1	1
Ex. B-I-4 (Tomb 2)	3	4	3
Ex. B-I-4 (Burial 3)	9	3	8
Ex. B-II-1	43	3	2 *3
-2	43		8
-3	15	1	3

*1 *Pachychilus* cf. *largillierti* (Phillipi, 1843), Figure 30b.
*2 *Pomacea flagellata* (Say, 1829), Figure 30a.
*3 *Neocyclotus dysoni* (Pfeiffer, 1852). One from each provenience unit.
*4 *Psoronaias* cf. *semigranous*, at least one, Figure 30c.

Figure 31.   ARCHITECTURAL DECORATIVE STUCCO ELEMENTS FROM INSIDE TEMPLE 3, MOUND 1, GROUP C.

STUCCO

Decorative Stucco Elements

Five thick, modeled, lime stucco fragments (Fig. 31) were collected from inside Temple 3 of Mound 1 in Group C. Two have rectilinear crosshatched elements. Two others are the tips of scrolls, one with outlining band. A single fragment is of a straight projection, with outlining bands. All are parts of the modeled stucco architectural decoration which anciently covered the interior and exterior of the temples. This well-known decorative technique of the Maya was especially well developed in the Middle Usumacinta during the Late Classic period.

BONE

Carved Bones

Anthropomorphic figurine fragment (Fig. 32a). A small piece of tubular long bone is carved into a small male human figurine with head, lower leg, and feet missing (found on the surface near the rear of the cave floor). The figure is standing with the legs together and the arms at his sides, the elbow bent at a right angle; the missing hands were apparently over belly. The figure wears a necklace or ruff around the neck and a broad belt around the waist. Two plain parallel upper arm bands are indicated on the right bicep. A trace of red paint can be seen on the ruff and along the edges of the loincloth. Length 4.9 cm, width 1.85 cm, thickness 0.4 cm.

A second fragment of carved bone found on the surface of the cave floor between Excavation Unit B and the cave wall appears to represent the lower arm and doubled-up fist of a human being

Figure 32.   CARVED BONE
a. fragment of a human figurine; *b.* human lower arm and fist.
a. Cave floor, rear; *b.* cave floor between Excavation
Units A and B and cave wall. Natural size.

(Fig. 32b). A plain parallel double band encircles the wrist and supports a round motif divided by a lazy Z design. This is almost identical to the bands and knot on Glyph 569 or the "Tied Pouch" found frequently on texts on carved monuments of nearby Yaxchilan, Tikal, and Naranjo (Thompson 1962). Length 3.5 cm, width 1.15 cm, thickness 1 cm.

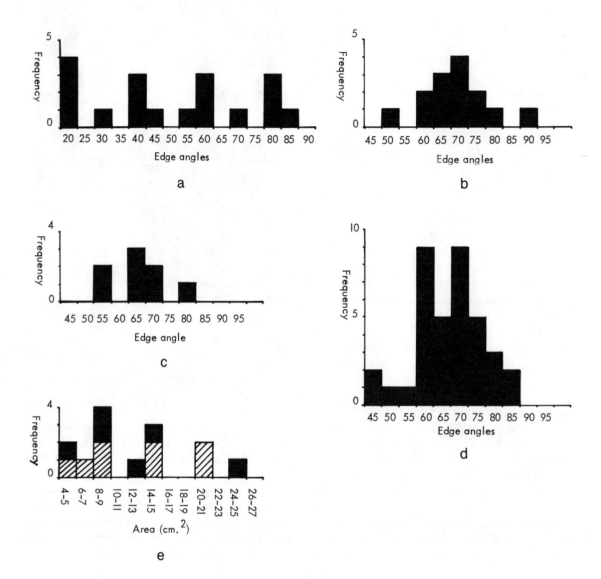

Figure 33.   EDGE ANGLE FREQUENCIES AND AREAS OF LITHIC ARTIFACTS
a. edge angles of utilized flakes; *b*. edge angles of notches; *c*. edge angles of denticulates; *d*. edge angles of scrapers;
e. areas (cm²) of notches; hatchured blocks indicate complete pieces; solid blocks indicate broken pieces.

SAN PABLO CAVE LITHIC ARTIFACTS

ARTIFACT TYPES

In two of the excavation units (B-I, B-II) in San Pablo Cave there is definite evidence of vertical mixing in the form of intrusive burials extending to the lowest excavated levels. In the third excavation unit (A), retouched chipped stone artifacts were so infrequent (Table 3) as to render adequate determinations of change over time impossible. Largely because of the mixed and indeterminate nature of the deposits it makes sense to review first the retouched tools from all levels and then deal with indicators of temporal span and change over time.

One of the most striking characteristics of the assemblage in all levels is the presence of relatively large flakes. Many of these are billet flakes and apparently derive from manufacturing activities, although one of the largest flakes (7 x 10 cm) has been transformed into a finely-made side scraper. Some commentary is warranted regarding some of the types because of peculiarities with the classification. Types not commented upon conform to standard definitions and usage.

Utilized Flakes

The only thing of note regarding this category is that a histogram of edge angles reveals a polymodal curve (Fig. 33a) indicating that the taxon is a composite one, comprising several functional tools, with a variety of cutting and woodworking functions.

Notches (Fig. 34a–c)

Only 3 of the 15 notches were formed by a series of small flake removals to create the concavity. The others were all simple, single flake removals, a few of which may have been fortuitous. One notch from BI-4 had a burinated edge, although it was impossible to determine if the burin blow was intentional. Notches form a normally distributed population on the basis of edge angle measurements (Fig. 33b), although

area measurements (Fig. 33e) for the group are more discontinuous, possibly a result of the small sample size. The fact that the range and mode of angle edges is nearly the same as that of the scrapers and denticulates, underscores the functional similarity of most of these implements.

Denticulates (Fig. 34d–f)

Only 1 of the 9 denticulates had large concavities formed by small flake removals. Denticulates varied considerably in the diameter of the constituent concavities, although edge angles appear to follow a normal distribution (Fig. 33c).

Cog Denticulates (Fig. 34g, h)

I have created this classification because of the distinctiveness of this type of tool and because several specimens seemed to form a relatively tight attribute cluster defining the type. Further investigation may show that the type is unimportant in a broader context, but the distinctiveness of these specimens merits their description as a separate type for this site. The specimens are round or sub-round, with wide concavities extending more or less around the perimeter, giving them a "cog" appearance. The specimens are much larger than other denticulates (27, 30, and 42 cm^2, as opposed to the largest normal denticulate, with an area of 16 cm^2). In addition to this, two of the three specimens were made of vein quartz cobbles that were either naturally flat and flaked around the perimeter, or split and flaked inversely. Because of the significantly greater size and mass of these implements, it is reasonable to infer that they were probably used for heavier work than the smaller varieties; one possible use is the rough trimming or shaping of wooden shaft implements. Edge angles (65, 65, and 70 degrees) and shape support this probability. The large scrapers with large end notches (to be described next) probably filled a similar, if not identical, heavy-duty role.

51

Table 3. Lithic Tool Frequencies by Excavation Unit

Tool Type	EXCAVATION UNIT											Total
	B-I-1	B-I-2	B-I-3	B-I-4	B-II-1	B-II-2	B-II-3	B-II-4	A-1	A-2	Tomb	
utilized flakes	7	1	4	—	1	1	4	2	1	—	—	21
notches	2	1	5	1	—	—	—	3	2	—	1	15
denticulates	1	1	—	—	1	2	2	—	—	1	1	9
cog denticulates	—	—	1	1	—	—	1	—	—	—	—	3
convex side scraper	1	3	3	—	1	—	4	3	—	—	1	16
straight side scraper	1	—	1	—	—	3	1	—	—	—	—	6
perpendicular scraper	—	—	2	1	—	—	—	—	—	—	—	3
scraper with thinned or retouched back	—	2	—	—	—	—	—	—	—	—	—	2
convergent scraper	—	—	—	1	—	—	1	—	—	—	—	2
double side scraper	—	1	3	—	—	1	1	—	—	—	—	6
raclette	—	2	—	—	—	—	—	—	—	—	—	2
perforator	—	—	—	—	—	—	1	—	—	—	—	1
burinated pieces	—	—	—	3	—	—	—	—	—	—	—	3
burin spalls	1	—	1	1	—	—	1	—	—	—	—	4
battered piece	1	1	—	—	—	—	—	—	—	—	—	2
alternately retouched piece	2	—	1	—	—	—	—	—	1	—	—	4
point/knife	—	—	1	—	—	—	—	—	—	—	—	1
crude biface	1	1	6	—	—	—	1	—	—	—	—	9
thin biface	—	—	4	1	—	1	1	—	—	—	1	8
crude blade	3	—	6	—	4	3	3	—	3	1	—	23
prismatic flint blade	—	—	—	—	—	—	—	—	—	2	—	2
prismatic obsidian blade	3	2	—	1	3	1	1	—	—	1	—	12
pebble chopper/ core	3	3	1	1	1	—	1	—	—	1	—	11
broken pebble	3	1	5	1	7	5	3	—	—	—	—	25
thin battered pebble	—	—	—	—	—	1	—	—	—	—	—	1
pebble core	—	—	3	—	—	—	—	—	—	—	—	3
miscellaneous core	—	1	—	—	—	1	—	—	—	—	—	2
crude conical core	1	—	—	—	1	—	—	—	1	1	—	4
other	—	pumice	pumice	—	pumice (3)	—	ochre	—	—	—	—	
TOTAL CHIPPED STONE	30	20	47	12	19	19	26	8	8	7	4	200

Figure 34. Notches and Denticulates
a–c. notches; *d–f.* denticulates; *g–h.* cog denticulates. Natural size.

Scrapers (Fig. 35)

Of note among the scrapers was an unusual combination of relatively large side-scrapers with a definite, large notch at one end (Fig. 35*a*, *b*). Three examples of this type were found, although they may have not been isolated as a distinct taxon. *Double-side scrapers* were generally of the convex/concave type, although there was one double concave scraper and one double convex scraper (Fig. 35*c*). *Perpendicular scraper* refers to scrapers on the distal or proximal edges of a flake (Fig. 35*d*). All examples from San Pablo were on the distal end; 1 was concave, the other 3 were convex. One scraper had a retouched back, and one other had a ventrally thinned back. There are two examples of convergent scrapers (Fig. 35*e*). Edge angles for all scrapers form a bimodal curve (Fig. 33*d*), although the peaks are so close together that the bimodality may well be the result of chance or recording variations. A larger sample, especially of the numerically inferior scraper subtypes is required to determine whether the distribution is definitely bimodal.

Raclette (Fig. 36*a*)

Two small, relatively thin flakes with small but continuous retouch along a lateral edge. The retouch is very regular and is clearly intentional. These specimens, therefore, most resemble what French prehistorians refer to as raclettes, and I have retained the name in this analysis.

Perforator (Fig. 36*b*)

A single example occurred in the San Pablo assemblage, although perforators occur consistently in other assemblages such as that of Coneta. Perforators are intentionally fashioned small tips on the edges of flakes. They often display abrasive microscopic use-wear, and they can support considerable pressure.

Burinations and Burin Spalls (Fig. 36*c*, *d*)

There was no definite classic burin in the assemblage; the high incidence of burinated pieces and burin spalls, however, including 1 classic burin spall, leave little doubt that burins were being intentionally manufactured at the site. It is difficult to be certain as to which artifacts were intentionally given a burin blow and which were accidentally burinated.

Battered Pieces (Fig. 36*e*,*f*)

One of these pieces made from obsidian is small (1 cm) and polyhedral; it is battered on two opposing edges as if it was a small bipolar core (Fig. 36*e*). It is very diminutive for a bipolar core, however, and no flake scars could be seen coming off from the battered edge. This piece is of considerable interest because of the chunky nature of the bit which recalls the obsidian industry in the Ocos and Barra assemblages (Clark and Lee 1984: 236–238). An even stronger hint at the Preclassic origin of this piece comes from the material itself, obsidian with numerous small, gray, round inclusions. This is the dominant type of obsidian used during Ocos and Barra phases in coastal Chiapas, and a cache of the material with small chunky forms was recovered from a Late Preclassic context at Izapa. The source for this unusual obsidian is probably Tajumulco, Guatemala (see Tables 8 and 9). Another piece is simply a flake with one edge lightly battered; again, no major flake scars occur along the battered edge. A third piece of unknown use is made on a long thin pebble (Fig. 36*f*).

Points (Fig. 36*g*, *h*)

The two points appear to be variants of a single type: elongated, broadly side-indented to the extent of resembling shouldering, leaving a slight-to-pronounced expanding base. Given the size and mass of these points, they were probably not projectile points but hafted knives, possibly used in a similar fashion to the other finely made quartz bifaces. The smaller specimen is quartz and the larger one is chert. In terms of workmanship, thickness, and overall dimensions, both points fit perfectly into the class of thin quartz bifaces to be described below, the only difference being the basal indentations and stems. It would therefore appear that the production of thin bifaces was only one stage in the manufacture of these points.

These specimens are not exactly comparable to any point types described in the literature. One's first impression is of an Archaic point, although straight and expanding stemmed long-bladed points continued to be made in the Maya Lowlands until Late Classic and Postclassic times (Willey 1972: 175). Willey (1972: 163) illustrates one point from Altar de Sacrificios which has a

Figure 35.   SCRAPERS
a, b. large side scrapers; *c.* double side scraper; *d.* perpendicular scraper; *e.* convergent scraper. Natural size.

relatively similar base, although the blade is shorter and the material is different; it is of the Terminal Classic or Early Postclassic. Kidder (1946: Pl. 24*n*) illustrates a small point with approximately the same base characteristics from the Classic period at Zacualpa. Both of these Maya analogues, however, are unique at the sites and may be from earlier occupations.

Elsewhere, MacNeish (1958: 66) illustrates a Palmillas corner-notched point from Tamaulipas which has the same general characteristics as the San Pablo point. The Palmillas point is from the Almagre Phase (ca. 200 B.C.). Even further afield, in Arkansas and the Mississippi Basin, the Table Rock point is of the same size and general shape as the San Pablo points and dates from 1500 B.C. and earlier (Hughes 1972).

Figure 36.   MISCELLANEOUS CHIPPED STONE ARTIFACTS
a. Raclette; *b.* perforator; *c–d.* burin spalls; *e–f.* battered pieces; *g–h.* points. Natural size.

Given the relatively low stratigraphic position (Level 3) of one specimen (provenience is not available for the larger specimen) and its overall aspect, one is tempted to place these points in the Late Archaic. However, some of the most similar point types in the literature are geographically very distant from the Peten, and general expanding stemmed points do appear to continue into the Postclassic period in the Peten. Willey even indicates that such forms are exclusively Late Classic or Postclassic for the Peten. The points from San Pablo are probably also Late Classic or Postclassic.

Crude Bifaces (Fig. 37*a–c*)

With one exception, all the crude bifaces that are complete enough to identify form are of the cordiform variety. The exception is more of a quarter circle shape, and may be a refashioned cordiform. An unusually high percentage of

Figure 37.   BIFACES
a–c. crude bifaces; *d–g.* fragments of thin bifaces. Just slightly less than natural size.

these tools was recovered in an unbroken condition which may indicate their manufacture at the site for some use at the site. Many have remaining patches of pebble cortex, and half of all specimens are quartz. Among the whole cordiform bifaces, there appears to be an unusual degree of standardization. All three specimens are 8.2 cm long. Width is more variable, as is thickness (Table 4).

Thin Bifaces (Fig. 37*d–g*)

None of these tools was whole, indicating that they were probably used away from the site and were only left at the site either because that was the place of manufacture (broken specimens were left behind, while good ones were taken away), or because the cave was the place of replacement of broken, probably hafted, items. These tools are finely crafted and display a relatively high attainment in the flintworker's craft. They were undoubtedly fabricated with billet flaking and/or indirect percussion. The quartz examples are especially fine, considering the medium. In fact, this class of tools is remarkable for the unusually high percentage of items made of quartz. All the quartz specimens have ovate forms while the flint specimens are either indeterminate or have angular corners or tips, indicating that they are probably a different type. Dimensions are moderately uniform, and thickness is always inferior to that of whole crude bifaces (Table 4). These thin bifaces were probably hafted, and possibly used as knives. As already noted, the single "point" base recovered from the site, fits very nicely into this category in terms of workmanship, material, and dimensions, except that it is shouldered. Because of the copious amount of debitage, especially billet debitage and debitage with cortex, and because of the prevalence of thin biface fragments, it is tempting to view San Pablo Cave as a manufacturing site for these items, at least during part of its occupation. This will be discussed further in the conclusions.

Pebble Chopper/Cores (Fig. 38a–c)

One of the more numerous artifact types was the pebble chopper/core. As the taxon implies, it was extremely difficult to tell whether these artifacts had been fashioned as tools in their own right or were simply cores from which flakes were derived. Equally good arguments can be presented for their use as choppers or cores. Most of these implements were made of quartz pebbles. Small pebbles from which several flakes have been removed indicate that even very small pebbles could be used as cores, possibly simply to obtain a sharp edge for butchering or other skin cutting. Other pebbles have simply been broken, and it seems unlikely that they were used as a source of flakes. Both of these extremes have been classified as separate taxons. Most pebbles were unifacially flaked; bifacial flaking was uncommon.

Table 4. DATA ON BIFACIAL ARTIFACTS

Level	Shape	Material	Length	Width	Thickness	Edge Angle
CRUDE BIFACES						
B-I-1	side fragment	chert	—	—	18	60
B-I-2	cordiform	chert	8.2	6.2	18	45–70
B-I-3	cordiform	chert	8.2	5.2	23	45–65
B-I-3	cordiform	quartz	8.2	4.6	19	45–70
B-I-3	quarter circle	quartz	6.0	5.7	23	60
B-I-3	side fragment	quartz	—	—	—	60
B-I-3	side fragment	chert	—	—	—	75
B-I-3	corner fragment	quartz	—	—	13	50–70
B-II-3	cordiform	quartz	—	4.6	16	50
THIN BIFACES						
B-I-3	ovate	quartz	—	3.3	8	65
B-I-3	side fragment	chert	—	—	7	45–55
B-I-3	ovate	quartz	—	3.5	8	65
B-I-3	ovate	quartz	—	3.1	10	45–60
B-I-4	ovate	quartz	—	3.7	9	60–70
B-II-2	right angle corner	chert	—	—	6	55
B-II-3	ovate	quartz	—	3.5	11	60
Tomb	pointed tip	chert	—	—	8	55
POINT/KNIFE						
B-I-3	stemmed point	quartz	—	3.3	8	70

Figure 38. PEBBLE CHOPPER/CORES AND CHERT CORES AND BLADES
a–c. choppers; *d–f.* chert blade cores; *g–k.* chert blades. Natural size.

Broken Pebbles

These were usually quartz pebbles which had a simple clean break, often just a cobble broken in two. They may have been used as planes or other tools, but they bear no retouch. They are somewhat enigmatic and common.

Pebble Cores (Fig. 38d–f)

Diminutive pebbles which showed clear evidence of having been worked, usually with only two or three flakes removed, were classified as pebble cores. They do not exhibit working edges of any quality, and the fact that some of them are very small quartz pebbles makes it seem unlikely that they were used simply to obtain a sharp-edged flake for breaking skin, or other similar work. It is still enigmatic why such small pebbles should be chosen when larger, more easily-worked materials were available in abundance, not only from the nearby river bed, but also in the rich deposits of the cave floor.

Crude Bladelets (Fig. 38g, h, j)

These comprise both blades and bladelets. Almost all examples are probably fortuitous; they lack the signs of intentional production. Where artifacts are plentiful, they do not comprise more than 3 percent of the assemblage, also indicating that they are probably fortuitous.

Prismatic Flint Blades (Fig. 38i, k)

Unexpectedly, 2 excellent examples of flint prismatic blades were recovered, 1 being an out-repasse (plunging) blade that carried the bottom of the core along with it. They were probably made by indirect percussion (John Clark, personal communication).

Prismatic Obsidian Blades (Fig. 39)

Fourteen fragments of these blades were found. Nine artifacts were medial sections, and only 5 were proximal ends. Interestingly enough, no distal segments were recovered. This same distribution of blade segments has also been noted in the colonial lithic industry of eastern Chiapas (Hayden 1976a). This may indicate intentional removal of the distal (usually curved) blade fragments at the manufacturing site prior to shipment or use. The 4 proximal ends consisted of 3 specimens with pointed platforms, which are generally considered most characteristic of the Late Preclassic (Tolstoy 1971: 274; MacNeish, Nelken-Turner, and Johnson 1967: 18, 22–25), and one larger platform, which was not ground and thus might be attributed to almost any ceramic time period. There was one medial fragment fashioned of green obsidian, indicating some connection with the Pachuca mines of Central Mexico. See Table 9 for the analysis of trace

Figure 39.   Prismatic Obsidian Blade Fragments
a–c. proximals; d–h. medials. Natural size.

elements and the identification of the source of four of these specimens.

Billet Flakes (Fig. 40)

Billet flakes were unusually common in the debitage at San Pablo Cave, and they were used as primary flakes for making retouched tools only rarely. It may well be that the thinness of this class of flakes rendered them too fragile for most tasks in which retouched tools were used. Taken as a whole, 12 percent of all flakes at San Pablo Cave exhibited definite signs of billet percus-

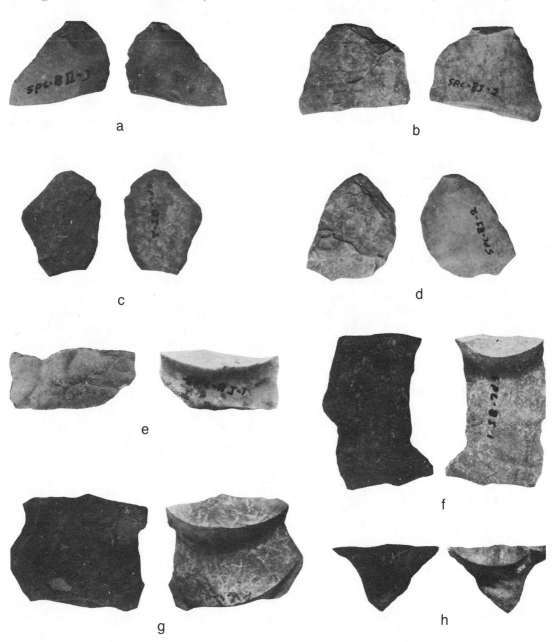

Figure 40.   DORSAL AND VENTRAL VIEWS OF BILLET FLAKES
a–d. type A; *e–h.* type B. Natural size.

sion. The actual number of billet flakes in the assemblage is probably almost double this figure since 44 percent of the flakes could not be identified with certainty as to production technique due to the lack of bulbs of percussion or other diagnostics. Of the 181 definitely identified billet flakes, 68 (5 percent of the total assemblage) had distinctly ground platform edges. I am aware that the distinctiveness or the identifiability of the billet flakes has been disputed (Mewhinney 1964). While there may be some overlap in the range of characteristics, I am convinced that in many cases billet flakes can be isolated with a relatively great degree of confidence. The characteristics I have used for identifying billet flakes are thinness, expanding form, ground platforms, pronounced lipping at the bulb, lack of distinct bulb of percussion, small platforms, or, alternatively, very large platforms, and in the case of the latter, "profiles." Two extreme types of billet flakes can be identified. The first (Type A) is the classical type which is thin, expanding, and has a small platform (Figs. 40a–d). The second (Type B) has a wide, thick platform almost forming a break (and indeed the flake has been broken off by the force of the billet, rather than flaked off), but which continues on over the face of the core or biface, giving an "r" shape to the side profile (Fig. 40e–h). These latter flakes can be very thick, characteristically near the striking platform. Not all flakes identified as billet flakes exhibited all the characteristics listed above. When a flake exhibited a large enough number of the characteristics in a distinct enough form to render classification as a billet flake very probable, it was recorded as a billet flake.

MATERIAL AND TECHNICAL CONSIDERATIONS

Since so much disturbance had taken place in the major excavation units, and since diagnostic tools were mixed at various levels, I attempted to determine if there remained any perceptible stratigraphy, or change over time, in the manner of working stone and in the choice of raw materials. Consideration of all lithic artifactual materials (as opposed to only the modified tools) provided an adequate basis for statistical comparisons, and I hoped that on a statistical basis some trends

over time might still be partially coherent, and might even provide a basis for determining which levels corresponded to which general time periods. Toward that end, raw materials, the extent of cortex coverage, and the detachment techniques were recorded for each flake, and proportional frequencies were derived for each level and each excavation unit. Tool debitage ratios were also calculated for the same assemblages. The results are presented in Tables 5–7.

RAW MATERIALS

Raw materials were, for the most part, probably obtained from the rich cobble beaches along the Usumacinta adjacent to the cave, but especially the beach on the upriver side of El Cayo Island (Fig. 5). These are reportedly the richest cobble beaches within a hundred miles upstream or downstream (Thomas Lee, personal communication). Changes, therefore, in the major constituents of the assemblages (quartz and chert) probably do not reflect change in availability, but rather in preference. And it has been seen that quartz was distinctly preferred for some tool types. For present purposes, Excavation A will not be considered because of the very low artifact frequencies in several of its levels.

Two trends are perceptible in the data. Quartz reaches its greatest popularity in Level 2 while chert is lowest in popularity. Chert on the other hand, is most popular in the lowest level (4), decreases in popularity through Level 2, and regains some popularity in Level 1. Also of interest is the concentration of obsidian in the top two levels, possibly indicating Late Preclassic to Classic dates for one or both of these levels. There is no definite trend discernible in the fire-altered materials, although there tends to be slightly more in Excavation B-II than in B-I, probably indicating a placement of hearths more towards the inside of the shelter. Almost all of the fire-altered pieces were identified on the basis of potlidding, and were probably accidentally altered (Fig. 41a–d). A few pieces showed unmistakable signs of color and texture alteration, however, and may have been intentionally heat-treated. Many more texture-altered pieces probably were undetected in this analysis. At the very least, an unusual amount of fire activity is attested

Table 5. RAW MATERIAL PROPORTIONS BY LEVEL

Excavation Unit	Total Number	% Quartz	% Chert	% Chalcedony	% Obsidian	% Miscellaneous	Total Percent	% Fire-Altered
B-I-1	163	20	69	5	2	4	100	4
B-I-2	159	24	67	5	3	1	100	5
B-I-3	334	19	79	1	1	1	101	6
B-I-4	87	18	80	—	1	—	99	4
B-II-1	136	16	75	2	2	4	99	10
B-II-2	167	23	72	2	2	2	101	11
B-II-3	232	23	75	2	2	—	101	6
B-II-4	139	10	89	1	—	—	100	7
A-1	31	7	87	7	—	—	101	—
A-2	41	12	78	—	2	6	100	2
A-3	11	9	91	—	—	—	100	27
A-4	4	—	100	—	—	—	100	—

Table 6. DETACHMENT TECHNIQUE PROPORTIONS BY LEVEL

Excavation Unit	Total Number	% Direct Hardhammer Percussion	% Billet with Ground Platform	% Other Billet	% Pressure	% Bipolar	% Miscellaneous	Total
B-I-1	164	54	7	13	1	2	22	99
B-I-2	157	53	5	4	1	2	36	101
B-I-3	328	32	7	9	—	—	52	100
B-I-4	87	25	5	14	1	—	55	100
B-II-1	128	49	2	5	2	—	41	99
B-II-2	163	49	—	3	0.5	0.5	47	100
B-II-3	229	40	3	9	0.5	—	48	100.5
B-II-4	137	31	7	8	—	—	54	100
A-1	28	75	—	—	—	—	25	100
A-2	40	48	4	—	2	—	45	99
A-3	11	73	—	18	—	—	9	100
A-4	4	75	—	—	—	—	25	100

Table 7. PROPORTIONAL AMOUNT OF CORTEX COVERAGE BY LEVELS (IN PERCENTAGES)

Excavation Unit	Total Number	% No Cortex	% Cortex On Striking Platform Only	% Small Amount of Cortex	% About Half Cortex	%All Cortex	Total %
B-I-1	133	37	11	17	19	17	101
B-I-2	156	33	12	16	21	18	99
B-I-3	334	66	5	7	13	8	99
B-I-4	87	56	7	10	13	13	99
B-II-1	135	42	15	10	16	18	101
B-II-2	158	31	10	24	16	19	100
B-II-3	221	58	6	15	9	14	102
B-II-4	138	70	2	9	9	10	100
A-1	31	36	16	7	29	13	101
A-2	38	50	3	21	11	16	101
A-3	11	55	9	9	—	27	100
A-4	4	50	—	50	—	—	100

Figure 41.   MISCELLANEOUS LITHIC ARTIFACTS

a–d. fire-affected flakes showing potlid fractures; *e.* worked hematite nodule; *f.* pumice; *g.* bipolar core. Natural size.

to by these heat-altered pieces. Compared to other assemblages, the incidence of fire-altered pieces seems high.

There were few exotic materials. Most notable were the obsidians, including several pieces of obsidian with clastic impurities, popular in Ocos and Barra times, but which come from an unidentified source. Also included was one piece of green obsidian probably from central Mexico. The remaining obsidian may have come from El Chayal or other nearby sources. A few flakes were of hard limestone.

A small abraded pumice pebble and a worked hematite nodule (Fig. 41*e, f*) were also present in the San Pablo Cave collection and may have also been acquired anciently on the El Cayo Island beach as both materials are present (Thomas Lee, personal communication).

DETACHMENT TECHNIQUES

Unfortunately, large proportions of the assemblages could not be analyzed in terms of detachment techniques (Table 6). This was because many flakes lacked bulbs of percussion due to breakage or the bulbs of percussion were not distinctive enough to classify the flakes within a specific technological grouping. Because of the large proportion of indeterminate flakes, the trends evident in Table 6 have little definite meaning. Of note, however, is the occasional appearance of the bipolar technique. There were only a few definite examples of this stone working technique (Figs. 36*e, f*; 41*g*). Many more of the pebble quartz flakes may have been manufactured in this way, but due to the difficulty of analyzing quartz artifacts, no definite attribution could be made. Many pieces had right-angle platforms but lacked diagnostic battering. When distinct bulbs of percussion could be identified on these quartz flakes, it appeared as though they had been struck from pebbles almost like slices of salami, via hard hammer percussion. These were remarkably numerous, and I am at a loss as to how to interpret them due to their small size, their lack of retouch, and the evident small size of the nuclei. The only suggestion for function is that these flakes may have been removed for use in some small cutting tasks.

One other item of technological note is the elevated proportion of billet flaking in these assemblages. As mentioned previously, these proportions can probably be doubled due to the high percentage of indeterminate flakes. It is noteworthy that a particular type of flint seems to have been selected for billet flaking of bifaces. This is a dark gray flint, varying from light gray to very dark gray, with small linear white fossils occurring throughout. Billet flakes of this material were sometimes very large, especially cobble decortication flakes. Billet flakes of quartz also occurred but were more difficult to identify.

CORTEX COVERAGE

Perhaps of more reliable significance are the trends evident in the amount of cortex left on flakes (Table 7). The idea behind the recording of these data was that workshop debris from the manufacture of core tools would tend to leave more flakes with more cortex, assuming that the

core tools were taken away from the site. If daily activities dominated at the site, primary flakes with good cutting edges would be sought and there would be higher proportion of flakes without cortex. Implicit in this classification was the possibility that the function of the site may have changed during its occupation. Some of the strongest trends from the site are evident in these figures. There is a distinct emphasis on flakes without any cortex in the lower levels (III and IV), while flakes with large amounts of cortex attain their greatest importance in the upper levels (I and II).

OBSIDIAN ANALYSIS

The obsidian samples from San Pablo Cave were selected to be further studied by trace element analysis to ascertain their source; these were chosen by John E. Clark. Clark first grouped all obsidian into postulated known and unknown source groups based on his own visual inspection (Table 8). Four samples were selected from these postulated sources to be further analyzed. A comparison of Tables 8 and 9 will

Table 8. SAN PABLO CAVE OBSIDIAN SOURCES*

	Pachuca	El Chayal	Tajumulco	San Martin Jilotepeque	Unknown
Ex. A-5-2		1			
Ex. B-I-1		2			
-2	1	1**	1		1
-3			3(1)	1(?)	
-4		1			
Ex. B-II-1		2		1	
-4		1			
Ex. B-II-4 (Tomb 2)		1			

*Identification by John E. Clark on visual inspection only
**Underlined samples were analyzed using the x-ray flourescence method by Fred W. Nelson, Jr.; see Table 9.

Table 9. TRACE ELEMENT ANALYSIS OF OBSIDIAN FROM SAN PABLO CAVE

Artifact Provenience	Form of Artifact	Rb ppm	Sr ppm	Zr ppm	Mno %	Fe_2O_3 %	TiO_2 %	Ba ppm	Na_2O %	Obsidian Source
Ex. B-I-2	Blade	144	14	109	.030	1.12	.074	178	3.73	Zinapecuaro
Ex. B-I-2	Blade	136	152	90	.094	.82	.144	971	4.17	El Chayal
Ex. B-I-4	Blade	137	153	91	.095	.83	.148	995	4.15	El Chayal
Ex. B-I-3	Chunk	90	197	192	.093	1.79	.182	1257	4.35	Tajumulco

demonstrate that his superficial judgment was essentially correct.

Table 9 presents the results of the trace element analysis carried out through X-ray flourescence on the four samples from San Pablo Cave by Fred W. Nelson, Jr., then of the Chemistry Department, Brigham Young University. A description of his methods of analysis can be found in Nelson et al. (1977) and Nelson, Sidrys, and Holmes (1978).

INTERPRETATIONS AND CONCLUSIONS

There are a number of reasons for seeing a basic change in the San Pablo Cave deposits between Levels I and II. The upper levels contain the bulk of the obsidian. It is also here that decortication flakes occur with their greatest proportional frequency; flakes without cortex are dominant in the lower levels. Curiously, the incidence of quartz materials becomes greater in the upper levels, whereas chert predominates in the lower levels. It seems probable that during the earlier times the cave was used more frequently as a habitation or stopover location. This would explain the emphasis on flakes without cortex at the lower levels. However, the unusually high percentage of billet flakes, the extensive heat alteration of flint materials, and the overall low tool-to-debitage ratio (Table 10) all indicate that the site was serving as a workshop even by its earliest occupants. The proximity of abundant raw material would also favor this interpretation. The paucity of bifacial pieces made of the gray chert, which constitutes the bulk of the billet flakes, also indicates that the pieces being manufactured with billets were taken away from the site and very few of them were brought back. The combined indicators point to a partly specialized function during early occupation (Mamom or Tzakol) and more intensive specialization for the later periods of the site occupation (probably Late Classic). The resurgence in the use of flint in Level I may reflect some production for export of the finely-made ceremonial laurel leaf knives with pointed tips during Late Classic times. Many such knives were excavated at Altar de Sacrificios (Willey 1972), whereas few appear in the artifact report on Piedras Negras (Coe 1965). This may indicate that the flow of goods of great-

est value was downriver, i.e., groups upriver had desirable goods; and San Pablo craftsmen made local specialties to obtain the more desired items. In turn, San Pablo groups would hold items of great worth and would receive local products from downriver in exchange for them but would not necessarily trade local San Pablo goods downstream. Obviously, there are many other possibilities for explaining this patterning, including skewed sampling. The above is offered only as speculation.

It is also probable that the site continued to be used for shelter by families (or more probably by groups of hunters or traders) into later times, as there is no dropoff in the tool-to-debitage ratios in these levels; in fact, the ratio increases slightly, which is somewhat the contrary of what someone would expect. It may be that the site was used equally if not more as a workshop during the period represented by Levels III and IV. It also seems that the ovate bifaces belong predominantly to the time period represented by Level III. Unfortunately, elsewhere in Mesoamerica biface types can occur in almost any level (MacNeish, Nelken-Turner, and Johnson 1967: 85, 90). The fine chert bifaces with angular tips or corners occur in Levels I and/or II. Prismatic flint blades occur exclusively in the upper levels. Other tools occur too infrequently to attribute

Table 10. LITHIC TOOL-TO-DEBITAGE RATIOS

Excavation Unit	Tool Debitage	Absolute Values
BI-1	.23	30:133
BI-2	.14	19:140
BI-3	.16	47:287
BI-4	.14	11:76
BII-1	.16	19:117
BII-2	.13	19:148
BII-3	.12	26:206
BII-4	.07	9:130
A1	.35	8:35
A2	.16	6:37
A3	less than .09	−:11
A4	less than .25	−:4
Tomb	.03	5:164
	TOTAL	1,671

them with any certainty to specific levels (given the mixed context), or they seem to occur uniformly throughout: e.g., utilized flakes, simple side scrapers. I strongly suspect, however, that the large cog denticulates belong almost exclusively to the earlier levels, together with the double concave/convex side scrapers; their distributions support the interpretation. Tool-to-debitage ratios are consistently higher in Excavation Unit B-II than in B-I, which probably reflects a greater tendency to use tools toward the front of the cave rather than the rear.

CONCLUSIONS

Caves, especially the rockshelter type, have long been recognized as man's most comfortable and efficient natural shelter. They immediately provide protection from the harsh elements, wild animals, and hostile human neighbors on five of six exposed sides, leaving only one direction which the occupants must watch over. Rockshelters have proven time and again to be not only the logical choice as the first homes of hunters and gatherers moving into a region, but they also have been used off and on ever since then as a temporary refuge. Therefore, they may contain evidence of human occupation of the region from the very first incursion into it by man as well as a lengthy, if broken, record of human use of it since then. It was this possibility that excited our imagination upon finding San Pablo Cave. Here, in the heart of the Lowland Maya culture area, was a rockshelter undisturbed, at least recently, which just might contain a long sequence of human occupation.

At the time the cave was found (and this still holds true for the interior forest Lowland Maya region or core area), no cultural remains could be securely dated before 900 B.C. (Willey, Culbert, and Adams 1967, Fig. 10; Adams 1971, Table 26; Sabloff 1975, Fig. 4; Gifford 1976, Fig. 8). The area was surrounded on the northwest, west, and southwest by different human occupations which were as much as 700 to 800 years earlier (now as much as 1,700 to 8,000 years earlier on the northeast; see Hammond 1977, MacNeish 1958, MacNeish et al. 1980). It was felt that the rockshelter might well contain culture-bearing deposits that went back as early as 900 B.C. or earlier.

TEMPORAL RELATIONSHIPS

Of course it is unfortunate that the test excavations in San Pablo Cave did not find undisturbed culture-bearing levels. We collected nothing specific which can be used to confirm MacNeish's off-hand evaluation of a 5000 B.C.

date for some lithic artifacts. The earliest ceramics in San Pablo Cave date to the Mamom horizon (600 to 300 B.C.). This phase is represented by four types and 16 percent of the ceramics recovered from the cave (Table 11). Ceramically, it is the second most heavily represented phase horizon.

Table 11. PERCENTAGE OCCURENCE OF NAMED CERAMIC TYPES, EL CAYO REGION

Phase	No. of Types	Frequency	Percentage
Mamom	4	74	15.5
Tzakol	8	306	64.0
Tepeu 1–2	6	40	8.4
Tepeu B	7	58	12.1
TOTAL	25	478	100.0

The following Lowland Maya horizon, the Chicanel, is not represented at San Pablo Cave. It appears that the cave was not inhabited or used from about 300 B.C. to perhaps A.D. 225. Throughout much of Chiapas this period is characterized by a change in population patterns, so it is not disturbing to find a lack of Chicanel occupation at San Pablo Cave. In general, it is a period of maximum ceremonial construction, though often of many small centers. More extensive excavations at El Cayo might produce evidence for this occupation, but all indications are that it would be limited to the central area.

The Early Classic Tzakol horizon, dating from about A.D. 225 through 525, is the time of the most intensive occupation at El Cayo. The ceramics of this period represent 66 percent of all ceramics from the cave (Table 11). While the Long Count inscribed dates from El Cayo are from over two hundred years later, it is to be expected that this civic/religious center was actively functioning much earlier, during the Early Classic period. It was, for instance, during this period that the major regional center of Yaxchilan, upriver, had its first long count date carved (Altar 13, 9.0.0.0.0., or A.D. 435, Hamblin and Pitcher 1980). The increased ceremonial activity in the general region indicates a rise in population density which may explain the maximum use of San Pablo Cave during this period.

The Tepeu 1–2 horizon (about A.D. 525–825) is the most weakly represented in San Pablo Cave. Only 24 sherds were found of this period or 5 percent (Table 11). None of the type-named ceramics appear to date to later than A.D. 700, which suggests a possible hiatus in human use of the cave during the Tepeu 2 horizon, or from about A.D. 700–825.

The following Tepeu 3 phase (A.D. 825–950) or Terminal Late Classic phase is poorly represented in the cave with only 12 percent of the ceramics (Table 11). Although the number of types remains almost constant, the frequency more than doubles the previous phase (Table 11). The re-emphasis in the cave's utilization is brief, for the end of Tepeu 3 marks the end of human use of the cave; no ceramics later than this period have been recognized. This, of course, equates well with abandonment of formal civic/religious centers throughout the Lowland Maya area at the end of the Late Classic period. The apparent end of human use of San Pablo Cave appears to be part of this general trend, for whatever causes.

Group B

This small group of structures on the flat low-lying valley bottom near the river's edge seems, on the basis of admittedly weak evidence, to have been first occupied in the Mamom horizon (600–300 B.C.) times, and to have been abandoned during the following Chicanel horizon. It was most intensively occupied during the Tzakol horizon (A.D. 255–550). Perhaps all or many of the structures visible now on the surface were built and abandoned during that horizon.

Group C

The earliest ceramic evidence collected in this principal structural group dates to the Tzakol horizon, but surely evidence of a Mamom occupation underlies some of these large structures. Jakeman (Lowe, personal communication, 1980) reportedly recovered Mamom-horizon ceramics from his pits near the outside base of the group. The Tzakol horizon is weakly represented as is the succeeding Tepeu 1–2 horizon. The lintel from El Cayo has a late Cycle 9 date (Table 12) which corresponds to about A.D. 751 with the 11.16 correlation, according to Hamblin and Pitcher (1980, Fig. 1, Appendix A) or A.D. 772 as originally published by Proskouriakoff (1950: 86). Stylistically, the lintel and two stelae (Table 12) from El Cayo all appear to date to between A.D. 741 and 810 (Proskouriakoff 1950: 186). These dates (and they must be very close to the real dates) all fall at the end of the Tepeu 2 horizon and are indicative of great building and sculpturing activity which is not reflected well in our superficial ceramic sample. Neither of the two Tepeu types collected date to this latest subperiod but instead to the Tepeu 1 horizon.

Tepeu 3 is the strongest ceramic phase represented in Group C, with almost 70 percent of the

Table 12. EL CAYO CARVED MONUMENTS

Carved Monuments	Maler 1903	Greene, Rands, and Graham 1972	Morley 1946: Table XII 11.16.0.0.0 Dates A.D.	Proskouriakoff 1950		(Kudlek 1977) Hamblin/Pitcher 1980, Vol. 45, No. 2
				Date	Style/Date	
Stela 1	Pl. 34, 1		$761 \pm (741-781)$		$9.16.10.0.0 \pm 2$ Katuns $761 \pm \frac{781}{741}$	
Stela 1	Pl. 34, 2		$810 \pm$		$9.19.0.0.0 \pm (?)$ $810 \pm$	
Stela 3	Fig. 31					
Wall Panel 1	Pl. 35 (Lintel 1)	Pl. 22, 772	$772 \pm \frac{802}{762}$	9.17.1.2.12	$9.17.10.0.0 \pm 2$ Katuns $782 \pm \frac{802}{762}$	9.16.0.2.16 751
Wall Panel 2		Pl. 23, 700–750				

few sherds recovered dating to this time. There are no ceramics in our collection which date later than A.D. 950 in Group C.

SPATIAL RELATIONSHIPS

The ceramic collections from El Cayo are of such limited size that they do not permit normal assignment to specific ceramic spheres under the strict but reasonable criteria established by Ball (1976: 323, 324). Since the El Cayo collections contain many types common to the different Lowland Maya ceramic spheres as originally defined by Willey, Culbert, and Adams (1967: 306–311), it is expected that the El Cayo zone should fall within the recognized spatial distribution of several such established ceramic spheres. I will indicate the probable ceramic sphere affiliation of each horizon represented since we cannot properly speak of ceramic complexes in the El Cayo zone based on the present material.

Mamom Horizon

The spatial distribution of the Mamom ceramic sphere as first defined at the Guatemalan Maya Ceramic Conference (Willey, Culbert, and Adams 1967: 308) included only a limited part of the core Lowland Maya area. El Cayo falls outside the boundaries of this original definition. Later, Ball (1976: 325) indicated that the western boundary of this sphere, the one which affects El Cayo, is in Tabasco at Tiradero and indeed includes a much wider area than the original description. This wider definition of the spatial limits of the Mamom ceramic sphere probably would include El Cayo. The presence of Muxanal Red-on-cream at El Cayo, a key diagnostic feature of this sphere, is in harmony with the more western distribution of this particular type of pottery.

Chicanel Horizon

There are no ceramics in the present study that can be dated to this horizon. The original distribution pattern of the Chicanel sphere includes the El Cayo zone and a larger ceramic sample from our site would probably show a Chicanel presence.

Tzakol Horizon

It seems clear that the El Cayo zone was well within the Tzakol ceramic sphere at this time. There are several characteristic ceramic features of this sphere at San Pablo Cave and some at Groups B and C. None of the several Tzakol sphere diagnostics which result from the influence of Teotihuacan on Lowland Maya culture are present in the collections from El Cayo.

Tepeu 1–2 Horizon

Again, the El Cayo zone falls within the boundaries of the Tepeu ceramic sphere as originally outlined. The lack of recognized ceramic types which continue on to the end of the horizon (i.e., A.D. 700–830), however, suggests that the breakdown and increased heterogeneity present in the following horizon had its beginning at this time. The exuberance and proliferation in polychrome types seen in the El Cayo zone parallel what was happening throughout the sphere in general, in spite of the fact that the Tepeu 1–2 horizon at El Cayo is the weakest of all horizons represented there.

During the Tepeu 2 horizon, El Cayo (Group C), according to Marcus (1976: 94), was a "tertiary" center dependent to Piedras Negras which in turn was dependent to Yaxchilan. It is most reasonable to expect that a small civic/religious center intermediate between much larger centers on a navigable river would be under the social, political, ceremonial, or religious hegemony of one of them. Apparently, Yaxchilan dominated Piedras Negras (ibid) for at least two short periods of time, A.D. 529–534 and A.D. 751–761. These two periods fall almost entirely within the Tepeu 1–2 horizons. El Cayo, because of its closer proximity downriver to Piedras Negras, may have been dependent to that center rather than to Yaxchilan farther upriver, but the difficulty of crossing the great rivers (most feasible, incidentally at El Cayo) must have been a factor in this situation

Tepeu 3 Horizon

During this horizon, the previous pattern of an all-encompassing ceramic sphere for much of the central part of the Maya Lowlands is broken, resulting in at least three separate spheres greatly limited in extent (Willey, Culbert, and Adams 1967: 310, 311; Fig. 9). The Boca sphere, which includes the area round Altar de Sacrificios and Seibal upriver on the Usumacinta and Pasion Rivers, is the closest to the El Cayo zone. This sphere distinction has been accepted by both Sabloff (1975: 17–19) and Adams (1971, Table 24) for their respective sites. Neither Sabloff, Adams, nor the original Guatemalan ceramic conference, however, describe the content of the Boca ceramic sphere.

Ball's (1976: 323, 324) refinement of the ceramic sphere definition and his suggested criterion for assignment of ceramic complexes to them helps resolve the problem of El Cayo affiliation. Ball emphasizes that the strength of a sphere relationship will vary from one site's ceramic complex to another and that the assignment of a particular ceramic complex to a specific site should depend more fully on the relative quantitative similarities between the two. He suggests that the relationship could be graded as one of three possibilities: full sphere association (Class 1), peripheral sphere membership (Class 2), or exclusion from a sphere (Class 3).

Using Ball's criterion, it is not only impossible to assign the poor Tepeu 3 ceramics from San Pablo in El Cayo to a ceramic sphere as now defined in the Maya Lowlands, but the correspondence between the two major sites of Altar de Sacrificios and Seibal in the nearest sphere, Boca, hardly justifies their inclusion in the same sphere. Based on the published record, I can find only three commonly shared types at the two sites, of which only one occurs in a high frequency. This is hardly enough resemblance to indicate that the two sites are part of one sphere, let alone to use it for the definition of that sphere.

SAN PABLO CAVE FUNCTIONS

In a famous article on the role of caves in Maya society by Thompson (1959), he gives the following as certain cave functions: sites of religious rites of different kinds; sources of *zahuyha* or virgin water; repositories of burials, cremations, and ossuaries; places of refuge in times of stress; places for storage of goods; and use as

pottery dumps. Thompson was talking specifically about deep, dark caves of difficult access, and not of the rockshelter-type of cave such as is San Pablo. Obviously, the deep, dark and often damp cave has no appeal as a place of residence for any length of time. Associated as they were in pre-Colombian Maya religion with the entrance to the underworld and the land of the dead, these caves were of natural interest for sacred activities.

San Pablo, on the other hand, is a rather large, well-lit room, open only on one side, but it may nevertheless have served some similar functions. The four burials (including the remains of 23 individuals) found in it indicate that it too may have been considered an entrance to the underworld and thus particularly satisfactory for this purpose. The destroyed condition of most of the burials and the presence of ceramics in the cave from the Mamom horizon may imply that its burial function began as early as that period. Certainly it was a well-established custom by the time the Early Classic "tomb" Burial 4, was placed there. The small tomb chamber was used several times, and contained parts of four individuals, at least two of which were teenagers (Appendix A). All age grades and both sexes were buried in the cave. The pathologies observed in the osteological material from the burials by Philip Walker (Appendix A, Table 13) include evidence of arthritis, well-healed fractures, and two periods of disease or dietary stress in one individual.

While we found no remains of permanent residences, several different lines of evidence indicate that San Pablo Cave was used, at least sporadically, over a long period of time as a temporary domestic shelter. Both the quantity and nature of the lithic remains suggest that the cave was used again and again as a temporary camp and lithic workshop. The proximity of the cave to the abundant raw materials on the large cobble beaches at the head of El Cayo Island and on the same bank downstream from the cave in front of Group C was undoubtedly the principal reason for its use in stone tool manufacturing activity. The cave was not, however, just a workshop site, as the faunal remains clearly indicate. The species found include deer (plus many other unidentified ungulates, possibly including the tapir), as well as dog, bird, turtle, iguana, and fish (Appendix A, Table 14). Many of the bones were split as though to extract the marrow. Frequently, also, the bones were burned, suggesting that this had resulted from human consumption within the cave. Substantial quantities of freshwater clam and snail shells (Table 2) are further evidence that the cave was a place of habitation; especially significant are the latter which have been altered for consumption. The dietary importance of the shellfish is emphasized by the fact that their shells came from all excavation units and all levels in the cave.

CLOSING STATEMENT

The very brief investigation made in the region of El Cayo, and particularly the small test excavations in San Pablo Cave, have brought into focus again the great need for archaeological research in the valley of the Usumacinta River. The limited material gathered and published here will, we hope, serve to orient future investigations by indicating some of the spatial, temporal, and functional characteristics of the area. We have done little more than describe what we found, and attempt to integrate this information with what is known for the immediately adjacent Maya Lowlands. We hope that what we have presented here will be useful in filling in the larger picture of this important and often forgotten area. The El Cayo zone is small in relationship to the famous sites of Yaxchilan and Piedras Negras but, no doubt, is typical of numerous small sites subject to these great centers.

Table 13. ESTIMATES OF AGE AT DEATH OF
INDIVIDUALS FROM SAN PABLO CAVE

Burial Number(s) or Provenience of Human Remains	Age Estimate	Criteria Used in Age Determination
1a	Adult, 40+ yrs. (?)	Severe osteoarthritis of the vertebral column
1b	Child, 7 yrs.	Mandibular third molar is unerupted; the crown is complete but lacks roots
2a	Adult, 16+ yrs.	Complete fusion of distal epiphysis of humerus
2b	Adult, 16+ yrs.	Complete fusion of distal epiphysis of humerus
2c	Child, less than 14 yrs.	Unfused proximal tibial epiphysis
3a,b,c,d	Adults	Four individuals represented by adult mandibular fragment and molars which exhibit moderate dental attrition
4a	Adult	Size and robusticity of long bone fragments
4b,c	Adult, 16+ yrs.	Complete fusion of epiphysis on femoral heads
West end of Tomb 2	Adult	Long bone and cranial fragments of a mature individual
Sample 5 Level III	Adults	Long bone fragments of at least two major individuals
Sample 5 Level III	Infant	Total length of tibial diaphysis is 60.2 mm.
Sample 5 Level II	Infant	Deciduous mandibular molar lacks roots; decidious mandibular lateral incisor is beginning to erupt
BII Level I	Adult	Cranial fragments of a mature individual
BII Level 2	Adult	Cranial fragments of a mature individual
BII Level 3	Mature Adult	Deep arachnoid digitations along frontal crest
BI Level 2	Adult	Mandibular fragment of a mature individual
BI Level 2	Child, 5 yrs. (?)	Fragment of Proximal radial diaphysis
BI Level 2	Adult	Mandibular fragment of a mature individual

Table 14. SEXUAL IDENTIFICATION OF
ADULT SKELETAL REMAINS FROM SAN PABLO CAVE

Burial Number or Provenience	Sex Assigned	Criteria Used in Sex Determination
2a	Male (?)	Long bone fragments from very large individual
3a	Male	Contour of supraorbital margins and robusticity of cranial fragments
3b	Male	Robusticity of cranial fragments; size of mandible and development of mental area
3c	Female	Size and robusticity of mandible
4a	Male (?)	Linea aspera is well-developed; maximum diameter of femoral head is 47 mm.
4b	Female (?)	Small size of long bone fragments
Sample 5 Level III	Male	Rugose cranial fragments; large mastoid process

APPENDIX A

ANALYSIS OF THE OSTEOLOGICAL REMAINS FROM SAN PABLO CAVE

by
PHILIP L. WALKER

HUMAN SKELETAL REMAINS

Remains from at least 23 individuals were recovered from excavations at San Pablo Cave. Four of the more intact skeletons were assigned burial numbers during the course of the excavations. Most of the remaining individuals are represented only by skull or long bone fragments. The dispersed nature of some of the human skeletal material suggests intrusion of burial pits upon each other. Tomb 2, for example, contained one relatively complete skeleton and the remains of three additional individuals scattered throughout its fill. Disturbance of the cave is also indicated by the fact that fragments from the same individual (left and right temporal bones) were recovered from Levels I and II of Excavation Unit A.

Because of the fragmentary nature of the material, it is impossible to determine precisely the age at death or sex of most of the individuals represented. Although the majority of the burials were adults, children and infants were also present (Table 13). Five of the seven individuals whose sex could be determined were males (Table 14). The relatively large proportion of males may reflect the fact that, in disturbed deposits like those at San Pablo Cave, the heavier, more resistent bones of males remain in large diagnostic fragments more frequently than do those of females.

Several individuals from the site were afflicted with pathological conditions (Table 15). The bodies of vertebrae from two different buri-

als possessed osteoarthritic lipping. Two long bones from the collection exhibited old, well-healed fractures. Hypoplastic lines on the teeth of Burial 2c indicate at least two episodes of disease or nutritional stress which interfered with enamel development.

Table 15. ANOMOLIES AND PATHOLOGICAL CONDITIONS PRESENT IN HUMAN REMAINS FROM SAN PABLO CAVE

Burial Number or Provenience	Anomolies and Pathological Conditions
1a	Severe osteoarthritic lipping of cervical vertebrae; well-healed fracture of shaft of fibula
2c	Maxillary central incisor possesses two moderately deep hypoplastic lines 6 and 8 mm. from the base of the crown; this tooth has pronounced lingual shoveling; a maxillary premolar from this individual also has hypoplastic lines
3c	Mandible has severe alveolar resorption in the molar and premolar region (height of horizontal ramus at the level of the mental foramen is 19.0 mm.)
3a, b, or d	Well-healed fracture of the right distal radius; the distal end of the radius has been displaced anteriorly producing some deformity; the anterior border of a twelfth thoracic vertebra
BII Level III	Deep arachnoid digitation in the area of the frontal crest; the frontal bone is exceedingly thin, having a thickness of 3.8 mm. in the area of the base of the frontal crest

FAUNAL MATERIAL

A total of 144 animal bone fragments were recovered from the cave (Table 16). Since comparative osteological collections were not available at the time this material was examined, an exact identification of species present was not possible. Of the identified fragments, 70 percent came from ungulates. Although the presence of *Tapirus* could not be totally ruled out, most if not all of this material consists of the remains of deer. Two species of deer were present: *Odocoileus virginianus* and a second smaller species, probably from the genus *Mazama*. Of the ungulate bone fragments, 24 percent showed evidence of having been burned. Almost all of the long bone shafts from deer were fragmentary. Some of these bones appeared to have been cracked or split lengthwise, possibly for marrow extraction.

Pieces of turtle bone, most of which were fragments of carapace and plastron, were distributed throughout the site. In comparison to the bones from ungulates, a relatively small proportion of the turtle bone (8 percent) is burned.

The jaw of an iguana, as well as several pieces of bird and fish bone, were also identified. None of this material was burned.

Table 16. Faunal Remains from San Pablo Cave
Frequency of Burned, in Parentheses, and Unburned Fragments

Species	Unit A Sample 2	Unit A Sample 5-1	Unit A Sample 5-3	Unit A Sample 5-4	B-I Level 1	B-I Level 2	B-I Level 3	B-I Level 4	B-II Level 1	Tomb 2 (fill)	Total Burned from All Levels	Total Unburned from All Levels
Deer					3	5 (3)	15 (1)	2 (1)	2	3 (2)	7	30
Unidentified Ungulate	4	2	(2)	3		2		3 (6)	1	3	8	18
Canis sp. (?)					1							1
Unidentified Bird				3				1				3
Turtle	3			1	9	4 (1)	2 (1)		1	2	2	22
Iguana		1										1
Fish						7						7
Unidentified Fragments		1			17	(1)	6 (7)	7 (1)		1 (4)	13	32

REFERENCES

ADAMS, RICHARD E. W.
1971   The Ceramics of Altar de Sacrificios. *Papers of the Peabody Museum of Archaeology and Ethnology, Harvard University*, Vol. 63, No. 1. Cambridge.

ALVAREZ DEL TORO, MIGUEL
1952   *Los animales silvestres de Chiapas*. Departamento de Prensa y Turismo, Gobierno del Estado, Tuxtla Gutiérrez.

1960   *Los reptiles de Chiapas*. Instituto Zoológico del Estado, Tuxtla Gutiérrez.

1963   *Miscelenea ornotilógica*. Instituto de Ciencias y Artes de Chiapas, Tuxtla Gutiérrez.

1964   *Lista de las aves de Chiapas: endémicas, emigrantes y de paso*. Instituto de Ciencias y Artes de Chiapas, Tuxtla Gutiérrez.

1971   *Las aves de Chiapas*. Gobierno del Estado, Tuxtla Gutiérrez.

BALL, JOSEPH W.
1973   Ceramic Sequence at Becan, Campeche, Mexico. Ph.D. dissertation, Department of Anthropology, University of Wisconsin, Madison.

1976   Ceramic Sphere Affiliations of the Barton Ramie Ceramic Complexes. In "Prehistoric Pottery Analysis and the Ceramics of Barton Ramie in the Belize Valley," by James C. Gifford, pp. 323–330. *Memoirs of the Peabody Museum of Archaeology and Ethnology, Harvard University*, Vol. 18. Cambridge.

1977   The Archaeological Ceramics of Becan, Campeche, Mexico. *Middle American Research Institute*, Publication No. 43. Tulane University, New Orleans.

BALL, JOSEPH W. AND E. WYLLYS ANDREWS V
1975   The Polychrome Pottery of Dzibilchaltun, Yucatan, Mexico: Typology and Archaeological Context. In "Archaeological Investigations on the Yucatan Peninsula," pp. 227–247. *Middle American Research Institute, Publication* No. 31. Tulane University, New Orleans.

BERLIN, HEINRICH
1956   Late Pottery Horizons of Tabasco, Mexico. *Carnegie Institute of Washington, Publication* No. 606, pp. 95–153 (*Contributions to American Anthropology and History*, No. 59). Washington.

BLOM, FRANS
1953   La selva lacandona y tierras colindantes, Chiapas, México. In *La selva lacandona: análisis arqueológico*, by Frans Blom and Gertrude Duby. Segunda Parte (1957). Editorial Cultura. Mexico City.

CHRISTENSEN, ROSS T., EDITOR
1956   *U.A.S. Newsletter*, No. 34 (April 30). University Archaeological Society, Brigham Young University, Provo.

CLARK, JOHN E. AND THOMAS A. LEE, JR.
1984   Formative Obsidian Exchange and the Emergence of Public Economies in Chiapas, Mexico. In *Trade and Exchange in Early Mesoamerica*. Kenneth G. Hirth, editor, pp. 235–274. University of New Mexico Press, Albuquerque.

COE, WILLIAM R.
1965   Artifacts of the Maya Lowlands. In "Archaeology of Southern Mesoamerica, Part 2," edited by Gordon R. Willey, pp. 594–602. *Handbook of Middle American Indians*, edited by Robert Wauchope, Vol. 3. University of Texas Press, Austin.

COMPAÑ PULIDO, ENRIQUE
1956   *Asi es la cuenca del Río Usumacinta o Mono Sagrado*. Compañía Editora Tabasqueña, S.A., Villahermosa.

DUBY, GERTRUDE
1974   Panorama general de la selva lacandona. In *Memoria de la primera conferencia regional de geografía de Chiapas*, pp. 195–202. Gobierno del Estado de Chiapas, (Mexico City).

ECHEAGARAY BABLOT, LUIS
1957   *La Cuenca del Grijalva-Usumacinta a escala nacional y mundial*. 2nd edition. Secretaría de Recursos Hidraulicos, Mexico City.

ECHEAGARAY BABLOT, LUIS ET AL.
1957   *Lo que ha sido y lo que puede ser el sureste*. 3 vols. Secretaría de Recursos Hidraulicos, Mexico City.

GIFFORD, JAMES C.
1976   Prehistoric Pottery Analysis and the Ceramics of Barton Ramie in the Belize Valley. *Memoirs of the Peabody Museum of Archaeology and Ethnology, Harvard University*, Vol. 18. Cambridge.

GREENE, MERLE, ROBERT L. RANDS, AND JOHN A. GRAHAM
1972   *Maya Sculpture from the Southern Lowlands, the Highlands, and Pacific Piedmont, Guatemala, Mexico, and Honduras*. Lederer, Street, & Zeus, Berkeley.

HAMBLIN, ROBERT L. AND BRIAN L. PITCHER
1980   The Classic Maya Collapse: Testing Class Conflict Hypotheses. *American Antiquity*, 45 (2): 246–267.

HAMMOND, NORMAN
1977   The Earliest Maya. *Scientific American*, 236 (3): 116–133.

HARTMANN, WALTER I.
1971   Introducción al cultivo de las orquídeas. Editorial Fournier, Mexico City.

HAYDEN, BRIAN
1976   Coxoh Early Colonial Lithics: Coneta, Chiapas. Ms., New World Archaeological Foundation, San Cristóbal de Las Casas, Chiapas.

1977   Stone Tool Functions in the Western Desert. In Stone Tools as Cultural Markers: Change, Evolution and Complexity, edited by R. V. S. Wright, pp. 178–188. Australian Institute of Aboriginal Studies, Canberra.

HUGHES, JACK, EDITOR
1972   Projectile Point Types of Texas and Bordering States. West Texas State University Anthropological Society, Canyon, Texas.

JAKEMAN, M. WELLS
1954   Letter/report dated June 7, 1954, on work accomplished under concession of March 15, 1954. "Informes tecnicos," Vol. VIII, No. 3. Consejo de Arqueología, Instituto Nacional de Antropología e Historia, Mexico City.

KIDDER, ALFRED V.
1946   Appendix C: The Artifacts of Zacualpa. In "Excavations at Zacualpa, Guatemala", by Robert Wauchope, pp. 158–167. Middle American Research Institute, Publication 14. The Tulane University of Louisiana, New Orleans.

KUDLEK, MANFRED
1977   Computer Printout of Dated Maya Monuments by Ceremonial Center. University of Hamburg, Hamburg.

LEE, THOMAS A., JR.
1963   Usumacinta River Reconnaissance, November 12 to November 22, 1963. Ms., New World Archaeological Foundation and the Departamento de Monumentos Prehispánicos, Instituto Nacional de Antropología e Historia, Mexico City.

1969   Second Usumacinta River Reconnaissance, November 29 to December 10, 1965. Ms., New World Archaeological Foundation and the Departamento de Monumentos Prehispánicos, Instituto Nacional de Antropología e Historia, Mexico City.

1979   The Uppermost Grijalva Basin: A Preliminary Report of a New Maya Archaeology Project. XIII Mesa Redonda: Balance y Perspectiva de la Antropología de Mesoamerica y del Norte de México (1973, Jalapa). Mexico City.

LEE, THOMAS A., JR. AND JOHN E. CLARK
1980   Investigaciones arqueologícas en la region Camcum-Canajaste, Colonia Las Delicias, Municipio La Trinitaria, Chiapas, México. Preliminary report submitted to the Consejo de Arqueología, Instituto Nacional de Antropología e Historia, Mexico City.

LOWE, GARETH W.
1959   The Chiapas Project, 1955–1958: Report of the Field Director. Papers of the New World Archaeological Foundation, No. 1 (Publication No. 3). Orinda.

MacNEISH, RICHARD S.
1958   Preliminary Archaeological Investigation in the Sierra Tamaulipas, Mexico. Transactions of the American Philosophical Society, n.d., Vol. 48, Part 6. Philadelphia.

MacNEISH, RICHARD S., ANTOINETTE NELKEN-TURNER, AND IRMGARD W. JOHNSON
1967   Nonceramic Artifacts. The Prehistory of the Tehuacan Valley, Vol. 2. Robert S. Peabody Foundation, Phillips Academy, Andover (University of Texas Press, Austin).

MacNEISH, RICHARD S., JEFFREY K. WILKERSON, AND ANTOINETTE NELKEN-TURNER
1980   First Annual Report of the Belize Archaic Archaeological Reconnaissance. Robert F. [sic] Peabody Foundation for Archaeology, Phillips Academy, Andover.

MALER, TEOBERT
1901   Researches in the Central Portion of the Usumacinta Valley: Reports of Explorations for the Museum, 1889–1900. Memoirs of the Peabody Museum of Archaeology and Ethnology, Harvard University, Vol. 2, No. 1. Cambridge.

1903   Researches in the Central Portion of the Usumacinta Valley: Report of the Explorations for the Museum, Second Part. Memoirs of the Peabody Museum of Archaeology and Ethnology, Harvard University, Vol. 2, No. 2. Cambridge.

MARCUS, JOYCE
1976   Emblem and State in the Classic Maya Lowlands: An Epigraphic Approach to Territorial Organization. Dumbarton Oaks, Trustees for Harvard University, Washington.

MARTINEZ VASQUEZ, VICENTE
1974   La selva lacandona: sus recursos naturales y su explotación racional. In Memoria de la primera conferencia regional de geografía de Chiapas, pp. 203–218. Gobierno del Estado de Chiapas (Mexico City).

MASON, J. ALDEN
1934   Maya Sculptures Rescued from the Jungle. Bulletin of the Panamerican Union, Vol. 68, No. 2, pp. 88–101. Washington.

1935   Preserving Ancient America's Finest Sculptures. The National Geographic Magazine, 68 (5): 537–570.

MEWHINNEY, H.
1964   Skeptic Views of the Billet Flake. American Antiquity, 30 (2): 203–205.

MIRANDA, FAUSTINO
1952   La vegetación de Chiapas. 2 vols. Departamento de
        Prensa y Turismo, Gobierno del Estado, Tuxtla
        Gutiérrez. (Cover only of second volume gives 1953
        as publication date.)

MORLEY, SYLVANUS G.
1946   The Ancient Maya. Stanford University Press, Palo
        Alto.

MÜLLERRIED, FEDERICO K. G.
1957   Geología de Chiapas. Departamento de Prensa y
        Turismo, Gobierno del Estado, Tuxtla Gutiérrez.

MUNSELL COLOR COMPANY, INC.
1954   Munsell Soil Color Charts. Baltimore.

NELSON, FRED W., KIRK K. NIELSON, NOLAN F. MANGELSON,
MAX W. HILL, AND RAY T. MATHENY
1977   Preliminary Studies of the Trace Element Compo-
        sition of Obsidian Artifacts from Northern
        Campeche, Mexico. American Antiquity, 42 (2):
        209–225.

NELSON, FRED W., RAYMOND V. SIDRYS, AND RICHARD D.
HOLMES
1978   Trace Element Analysis by X-Ray Fluorescence of
        Obsidian Artifacts from Guatemala and Belize. In
        'Artifacts,' by Gordon R. Willey, pp. 153–161. In
        "Excavations at Seibal, Department of Peten,
        Guatemala," edited by Gordon R. Willey, pp.
        1–189. Memoirs of the Peabody Museum of Archae-
        ology and Ethnology, Harvard University, Vol. 14,
        No. 1. Cambridge.

PROSKOURIAKOFF, TATIANA
1950   A Study of Classic Maya Sculpture. Carnegie Insti-
        tution of Washington, Publication 593. Washing-
        ton.

ROBLES, ANGEL
1982   La selva lacandona: migraciones y problemas
        derivados de sus limitaciones en cuanto a la tenen-
        cia. In Memorias gira prioridades nacionales: bos-
        ques y selvas en el desarrollo nacional. Unidecima
        Reunión la Selva Tropical, la Colonización, la Salud
        y el Bienestar Social, Palenque.

SABLOFF, JEREMY A.
1970   Type Descriptions of the Fine Paste Ceramics of
        the Bayal Boca Complex, Seibal, Peten,
        Guatemala. In "Monographs and Papers in Maya
        Archaeology," Papers of the Peabody Museum of
        American Archaeology and Ethnology, Harvard
        University, Vol. 61, No. 2, pp. 357–404. Cam-
        bridge.

1975   Excavations at Seibal: Ceramics. Memoirs of the
        Peabody Museum of Archaeology and Ethnology,
        Harvard University, Vol. 13. Cambridge.

SECRETARIA DE PROGRAMACION Y PRESUPUESTO (S.P.P.)
n.d.   Carta topográfica 1:250,000. Tenosique E15-9 and
        Las Margaritas E15-12, D15-3. Coordinación Gen-
        eral de los Servicios Nacionales de Estadística,
        Geografía e Informática, Mexico City.

SMITH, ROBERT E.
1955   Ceramic Sequence at Uaxactun, Guatemala. 2 vols.
        Middle American Research Institute, Publication
        20. Tulane University, New Orleans.

1958   The Place of Fine Orange Pottery in Mesoamerican
        Archaeology. American Antiquity, 24 (2): 151–160.

SMITH, ROBERT E. AND JAMES C. GIFFORD
1966   Maya Ceramic Varieties, Types, and Wares at
        Uaxactun: Supplement to "Ceramic Sequence at
        Uaxactun, Guatemala." Middle American Research
        Institute, Publication 28, pp. 125–174. Tulane Uni-
        versity, New Orleans.

THOMPSON, J. ERIC (S.)
1959   The Role of Caves in Maya Culture. In "Ameri-
        kanistische miszellen. Festband Franz Terner," ed-
        ited by W. Bierhenke, W. Haberland, V. Johansen,
        and G. Zimmerman, pp. 122–129. Mitteilungen
        aus dem Museum fur Volkerkunde, Vol. 25. Ham-
        burg.

1962   A Catalog of Maya Hieroglpyhs. University of
        Oklahoma Press, Norman.

TOLSTOY, PAUL
1971   Utilitarian Artifacts of Central Mexico. In "Archae-
        ology of Northern Mesoamerica, Part 1," edited by
        Gordon F. Ekholm and Ignacio Bernal, pp.
        170–296. Handbook of Middle American Indians,
        edited by Robert Wauchope, Vol. 10. University of
        Texas Press, Austin.

VELASCO COLIN, ROBERTO
1976   Los peces de agua dulce del Estado de Chiapas.
        Ediciones del Gobierno del Estado, Tuxtla Gutié-
        rrez.

WAGNER, PHILIP L.
1964   Natural Vegetation of Middle America. In "Natural
        Environment and Early Cultures," edited by
        Robert C. West, pp. 216–264. Handbook of Middle
        American Indians, edited by Robert Wauchope.
        Vol. 1. University of Texas Press, Austin.

WILLEY, GORDON R.
1970   Type Description of the Ceramics of the Real Xe
        Complex, Seibal, Peten, Guatemala. In "Mono-
        graphs and Papers in Maya Archaeology," Papers of
        the Peabody Museum of American Archaeology and
        Ethnology, Harvard University, Vol. 61, Part 4,
        No. 1, pp. 313–355. Cambridge.

1972   The Artifacts of Altar de Sacrificios. Papers of the
        Peabody Museum of Archaeology and Ethnology,
        Harvard University, Vol. 64, No. 1. Cambridge.

WILLEY, GORDON R., T. PATRICK CULBERT, AND RICHARD
E. W. ADAMS, EDITORS
1967   Maya Lowland Ceramics: A Report from the 1965
        Guatemala City Conference. American Antiquity,
        32 (3): 289–315.